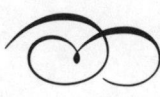

If Only I'd Said That: Volume II

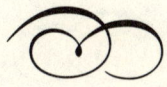

If Only I'd Said That: Volume II

Peter Legge

EAGLET PUBLISHING

Copyright © 2003 by Peter Legge

All rights reserved. No part of this book may be reproduced or transmitted in any form by any means without permission in writing from the publisher, except by a reviewer, who may quote brief passages in a review.

Eaglet Publishing
Peter Legge Management Co. Ltd.
4th Floor, 4180 Lougheed Highway
Burnaby, British Columbia, V5C 6A7 Canada
Tel. (604) 299-7311   Fax (604) 299-9188

National Library of Canada Cataloguing in Publication Data

Legge, Peter, 1942-
    If only I'd said that / Peter Legge.

Vol. 1 by Peter Legge with Duncan Holmes.
ISBN 1-55056-635-0 (v. 1). — ISBN 0-9695447-2-3
(bound: v. 2) — ISBN 0-9695447-3-1 (pbk: v. 2)

1. Success — Quotations, maxims, etc. 2. Conduct of life—Quotations, maxims, etc. I. Holmes, Duncan. II. Title.
PN6084.S78L435 1998   158   C 98-911051-6

First Printing   May 2003

Jacket design by Catherine Mullaly; cover photo by Hans-Ulrich Arnold; image manipulation by Debbie Craig
Typeset by Ina Bowerbank
Edited by Kim Mah
Printed and bound in Canada by Friesen Printers

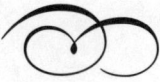

Other books by the Author

How to Soar With the Eagles
You Can If You Believe You Can
It Begins With A Dream
If Only I'd Said That
Who Dares Wins

Booklets

97 Tips on How to Do Business in Tough Times
97 Tips on Customer Service

Introduction

As a motivational speaker, much of my life has been devoted to searching out interesting stories, thought-provoking insights and the precious nuggets of wisdom that hold the power to uplift and inspire us. It's a lifelong passion that has had a profound influence on my own life — a passion that five years ago provided the impetus for a new book.

In 1998, I decided to compile some of the most inspirational things I had learned over the years in a book entitled *If Only I'd Said That*. A labour of love that I dedicated to the memory of my late father and mentor Bernie Legge, the thoughts contained in *If Only I'd Said That* clearly struck a chord with readers and in very short order it became a bestseller.

Since the book's release more than half a decade ago, I have met hundreds of people all over the world — politicians, teachers, business leaders, doctors, university professors, labour leaders, housewives — who have told me that they use the quotes and insights in my book in their own lives, whether speaking at a business meeting or graduation ceremony, or as a source of inspirational thought and encouragement for students, staff, family and friends.

In life you never know how what you do will impact on others. Recently, I was deeply moved by the story of a terminally ill woman who is using the insights contained in my book to help her find the words to tell her loved ones

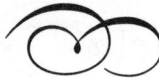

how much they have meant to her.

My good friend, author and fellow speaker Brian Tracy, says, "A single thought or idea at the right time can change the direction of your life." I believe this to be true. So, with the help of dozens of contributors, I am pleased to present *If Only I'd Said That: Volume II*, the best of the weekly insights that I have prepared for my staff and sent to hundreds of friends throughout the world.

I invite you to share these thoughts and insights with your family, your colleagues and your friends, and I sincerely hope they become the source of hope and happiness to you that they have been to me.

Vancouver, B.C.
Canada

June 2003

Part I

The Power of Relationships

A father's relationship with his son named Paco is broken.

After the son runs away from home, the father begins a long journey in search of him.

Finally, as a last resort, the father puts an ad in the local newspaper in Madrid. It reads: "Dear Paco, meet me in front of the newspaper office tomorrow at noon. All is forgiven. I love you."

The next day, in front of the newspaper office, there were 800 men named "Paco," desiring to restore a broken relationship.

Never underestimate the power of relationships in people's lives.

The Princess Cruises
10 Points of Service Credo

The Service Credo Will Be Known, Practised, Owned and Energized By All Crew

1. We strive to be the very best. We do the best job we are capable of all the time in every part of the ship, we are proud of what we do.
2. We react quickly to resolve passenger problems immediately. We do everything possible to please our passengers.
3. We smile; we are on stage. We always maintain positive eye contact and use our service vocabulary. We greet our passengers: we tell them "Certainly," "I will be happy to do so," and "It will be a pleasure."
4. We are friendly, helpful and courteous. It is the Princess way. We treat our passengers and fellow crew members as we would like to be treated ourselves.
5. We are ambassadors of our cruise ship, when at work and at play. We always speak positively, and never make negative comments.
6. Our uniforms are immaculate. We wear proper and safe footwear that is clean and polished, and we wear our nametags. We take pride and care in our personal grooming.

7. We are positive. We always find a way to get it done. We always try to make it happen. We never, never give up.
8. We use proper telephone etiquette. We always try to answer within three rings and with a smile in our voice. If necessary, we always ask if we may place customers on hold, and we eliminate call transfers whenever possible.
9. We are knowledgeable about all cruise ship information and always recommend the shipboard services.
10. We never say "no." We say "I will be pleased to check and see." We suggest alternatives. We call our supervisor or manager if we feel we cannot satisfy our passengers' needs.

Mothers

Somebody said a mother is an unskilled labourer . . . somebody never gave a squirmy infant a bath.
Somebody said it takes about six weeks to get back to normal after you've had a baby . . . somebody doesn't know that once you're a mother, "normal" is history.
Somebody said a mother's job consists of wiping noses and changing diapers . . . somebody doesn't know that a child is much more than the shell he lives in.
Somebody said you learn how to be a mother by instinct . . . somebody never took a three-year-old shopping.
Somebody said being a mother is boring . . . somebody never rode in a car driven by a teenager with a driver's permit.
Somebody said teachers, psychologists and pediatricians know more about children than their mothers . . . somebody hasn't invested her heart in another human being.
Somebody said if you're a "good" mother, your child will "turn out" . . . somebody thinks a child is like a bag of plaster of Paris that comes with directions, a mould and a guarantee.
Somebody said being a mother is what you do in your spare time . . . somebody doesn't know that when you're a mother, you're a mother ALL the time.
Somebody said "good" mothers never raise their voices . . . somebody never came out the back door just in time to see her child wind up and hit a golf ball through the neighbour's kitchen window.

*Somebody said you don't need an education to be a mother . . .
somebody never helped a fourth grader with his math.
Somebody said you can't love the fifth child as much as you love
the first . . . somebody doesn't have five children.
Somebody said a mother can find all the answers to her child-
rearing questions in the books . . . somebody never had a
child stuff beans up his nose.
Somebody said the hardest part of being a mother is labour and
delivery . . . somebody never watched her "baby" get on
the bus for the first day of kindergarten.
Somebody said a mother can do her job with her eyes closed and
one hand tied behind her back . . . somebody never
organized seven giggling Brownies to sell cookies.
Somebody said a mother can stop worrying after her child gets
married . . . somebody doesn't know that marriage adds a
new son or daughter-in-law to a mother's heartstrings.
Somebody said a mother's job is done when her last child leaves
home . . . somebody never had grandchildren.
Somebody said being a mother is a side dish on the plate of life
. . . somebody doesn't know what fills you up.
Somebody said your mother knows you love her, so you don't
need to tell her . . . somebody isn't a mother.*

Welcome to Holland

By Emily Pearl Kingsley

I am often asked to describe the experience of raising a child with a disability — to try to help people who have not shared that unique experience to understand it, to imagine how it would feel.

It is like this . . .

When you are going to have a baby, it's like planning a vacation trip to Italy. You buy a bunch of guidebooks and make your wonderful plans; the Colosseum, Michelangelo's David, and the gondolas of Venice. You may learn some handy phrases in Italian. It is all very exciting.

After months of eager anticipation, the day finally arrives. You pack your bags and off you go. Several hours later, the plane lands. The stewardess comes in and says, "Welcome to Holland." "Holland? What do you mean Holland? I signed up for Italy!" But there has been a change in the flight plan. They have landed in Holland and there you must stay.

The important thing is that they have not taken you to a horrible, disgusting, filthy place, full of pestilence, famine and disease. It's just a different place.

So you must go out and buy new guidebooks and you

must learn a whole new language and you will meet a whole new group of people you would never have met. It is just a different place. It is a slower place than Italy, less flashy than Italy, but after you have been there for a while and you catch your breath, you look around and you begin to notice that Holland has windmills, tulips and even Rembrandts.

But everyone you know is busy coming and going from Italy and they are all bragging about what a wonderful time they had there. And for the rest of your life you say, "Yes, that is where I was supposed to go and that is what I had planned."

And the pain of that may never go away because the loss of a dream is very significant. But if you spend your life mourning the fact that you did not get to Italy, you may never be free to enjoy the very special and very lovely things about Holland.

— Submitted by Siân Jones of South Wales

Trust Is the Foundation of All Relationships

The rule of thumb is simple — if your customers don't trust you; they won't buy from you. Trust is the glue that holds the business relationship together and is demonstrated repeatedly in your and your company's actions — what it does and doesn't do.

How To Build Trust
Trust is built over time through frequent interactions. In fact, any interaction you have with customers will either add or subtract from the trust factor.

Here are some simple things you can do to build trust:
- Return all phone calls immediately.
- Send thank-you notes.
- Be organized and dependable.
- Handle complaints promptly with empathy and honesty.
- Offer great customer service.
- Do what you say you are going to do.
- Show appreciation.
- Take time to understand your customers.
- Become a valuable resource to your customers.
- Create solutions that add value to customers.
- Partner with your customers.

- Create a customer, not a sale.
- Under promise — over deliver.
- Do something that is not expected.
- Always give more than is expected.

Do these things without any expectation of something in return. Always act in the best interest of your customers. Selling — in fact, doing business — is the process of building trusting relationships with people.

Action Recommendation:
Make it your challenge to find and implement at least three ways to build trust with customers this week.

Compliments of Joe McCracken
Royal Bank New Westminster Business Banking Centre

How Did We Survive?

Looking back, it's hard to believe that we have lived as long as we have. As children we would ride in cars with no seat belts or air bags. Riding in the back of a pickup truck on a warm day was always a special treat.

Our baby cribs were painted with bright-coloured lead-based paint. We often chewed on the crib, ingesting the paint. We had no childproof lids on medicine bottles, doors or cabinets, and when we rode our bikes we had no helmets. We drank water from the garden hose and not from a bottle.

We would spend hours building our go-carts out of scraps and then rode down the hill, only to find out we forgot the brakes. After running into the bushes a few times we learned to solve the problem.

We would leave home in the morning and play all day, as long as we were back when the streetlights came on. No one was able to reach us all day. We played dodgeball and sometimes the ball would really hurt. We ate cupcakes, bread and butter, and drank sugar soda, but we were never overweight; we were always outside playing.

Little League had tryouts and not everyone made the team. Those who didn't had to learn to deal with disappointment.

Some students weren't as smart as others or didn't work hard so they failed a grade and were held back to repeat the same grade. That generation produced some of the greatest risk-takers and problem solvers.

We had the freedom, failure, success and responsibility, and we learned how to deal with it all.

— *Author unknown*

The sucker born every minute is the sucker who believes that there's a sucker born every minute.

P.T. Barnum thought he had a finger on the pulse of the human psyche when he made his famous observation about a sucker being born every minute. And so he created a world that confirmed his beliefs. He gave what he assumed was a stupid public the "greatest show on earth," and he laughed at their gullibility.

The Barnum approach to the public lives on in today's media, which decrees that people want sensationalism, not quality, and which subsequently dishes out huge portions of tastelessness and mediocrity. But the truth is that quality can and does prevail, that when people are given the best they will respond to it and uplift their level of awareness accordingly.

What is your attitude towards quality? Do you demand the best from and for yourself and others? Or do you sometimes take the easy way out, sacrificing quality for quick-fix mediocrity?

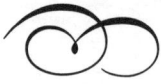

If I Knew

If I knew it would be the last time that
I'd see you fall asleep,
I would tuck you in more tightly and pray
the Lord your soul to keep.

If I knew it would be the last time that
I'd see you walk out the door,
I would give you a hug and kiss and call you back for one
more.

If I knew it would be the last time I could spare an extra
minute or two
To stop and say, "I love you," instead of assuming you would
KNOW I do.

If I knew it would be the last time I would be there to share
your day,
Well I'm sure you'll have so many more, so I can let just this
one slip away.

There will always be another day to say our "I love you's,"
And certainly there's another chance to say our "Anything I
can do's?"

But just in case I might be wrong and today is all I get,

I'd like to say how much I love you and I hope we never forget.

Tomorrow is not promised to anyone, young or old alike,
And today may be the last chance you get to hold your loved one tight.

So if you're waiting for tomorrow, why not do it today?
For if tomorrow never comes, you'll surely regret the day
That you didn't take the extra time for a smile, a hug, or a kiss
And you were too busy to grant someone,
What turned out to be their one last wish.

So hold your loved ones close today and whisper in their ear.
Tell them how much you love them and that you'll always hold them dear.
Take time to say "I'm sorry," "Please forgive me," "Thank you," or "It's okay."

And if tomorrow never comes, you'll have no regrets about today.

Meet Your "New" Boss

He's the toughest boss you'll ever have,
He's the only boss you'll ever have.

Your "new" boss is the toughest person in the world to please. If you don't do the job right, he'll get someone else. He always lets you know what he wants and he'll decide how much you get paid for it, but he's willing to pay whatever it's worth. If you do a great job, he'll always stand behind you. He's not concerned with what you did yesterday. It's what you do today that counts, so you can't get complacent. He's always interested in new products and services, but at the same time, he has a strong sense of loyalty.

Despite his tough attitude, he has no trouble getting people to work for him. In fact, he keeps more people employed than just about anyone else.

Your future is truly in his hands. As the real boss of everyone from the shipping clerk to the chairman of the board, he expects a lot from us, and he gets it. Best of all, each one of us can occasionally sit at this person's desk and see what it's like to be in charge.

Here's what you can do:
Recognize each of your customers as "the boss." Ask yourself if you are treating your customers just as you prefer to be treated when you are a customer. Remember that your

rewards in life will always be in exact proportion to the amount of service you provide for your customers.

— *from* The Unlimited Times
Joel H. Weldon & Assoc. Inc.

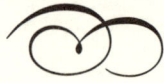

Keep Your Fork

There was a young woman who had been diagnosed with a terminal illness and had been given three months to live. As she was getting her things "in order" she contacted her Rabbi and had him come to her house to discuss certain aspects of her final wishes. She told him which songs she wanted sung at the service, what scriptures she would like read, and what outfit she wanted to be buried in.

Everything was in order and the Rabbi was preparing to leave when the young woman suddenly remembered something very important to her. "There's one more thing," she said excitedly. "What's that?" asked the Rabbi. "This is very important," the young woman continued. "I want to be buried with a fork in my right hand." The Rabbi stood looking at the young woman, not knowing quite what to say. "That surprises you, doesn't it?" the young woman asked. "Well, to be honest, I'm puzzled by the request," said the Rabbi.

The young woman explained, "My grandmother once told me this story and from that time on I have always tried to pass along its message to those I love and those who are in need of encouragement. In all my years of attending socials and dinners, I always remember that when the dishes of the main course were being cleared, someone would inevitably lean over and say, 'Keep your fork.' It was my favourite part because I knew that something better was coming — like

velvety chocolate cake or deep-dish apple pie. Something wonderful and with substance! So, I just want people to see me there in that casket with a fork in my hand and I want them to wonder 'What's with the fork?' Then I want you to tell them: Keep your fork, the best is yet to come."

The Rabbi's eyes welled up with tears of joy as he hugged the young woman goodbye. He knew this would be one of the last times he would see her before her death. But he also knew that the young woman had a better grasp of heaven than he did. She had a better grasp of what heaven would be like than many people would twice her age, with twice as much experience and knowledge. She knew that something better was coming.

At the funeral, people were walking by the young woman's casket and they saw the cloak she was wearing and the fork placed in her right hand. Over and over, the Rabbi heard the question, "What's with the fork?" And over and over he smiled. During his message the Rabbi told the people of the conversation he had with the young woman shortly before she died. He also told them about the fork and about what it symbolized to her. He told the people how he could not stop thinking about the fork and that they probably would not be able to stop thinking about it either. He was right.

The next time you reach down for your fork, let it remind

you, ever so gently, that the best is yet to come. Friends are a very rare jewel indeed. They make you smile and encourage you to succeed. They lend an ear, they share a word of praise and they always want to open their hearts to us. Show your friends how much you care. Remember to always be there for them, even when you need them more. For you never know when it may be their time to "Keep your fork." Cherish the time you have and the memories you share. Being friends with someone is not an opportunity but a sweet responsibility. And keep your fork.

— *Submitted by Bryan Locke, CA*
Wolf & Co.

Life Lessons

A water bearer had two large pots; each hung on the ends of a pole, which he carried across his neck. One of the pots had a crack in it, while the other pot was perfect and always delivered a full portion of water. At the end of the long walk from the stream to the house, the cracked pot arrived only half-full. For a full two years this went on daily, with the bearer delivering only one-and-a-half pots full of water to his house. Of course, the perfect pot was proud of its accomplishments; perfect for which it was made. But the poor cracked pot was ashamed of its own imperfection, and miserable that it was able to accomplish only half of what it had been made to do.

After two years of what it perceived to be a bitter failure, it spoke to the water bearer one day by the stream. "I am ashamed of myself, and I want to apologize to you. I have been able to deliver only half my load because this crack in my side causes water to leak out all the way back to your house. Because of my flaws, you have to do all of this work, and you don't get full value from your efforts," the pot said.

The bearer said to the pot, "Did you notice that there were flowers only on your side of the path, but not on the other pot's side? That's because I have always known about your flaw, and I planted flower seeds on your side of the path, and every day while we walk back, you've watered them.

"For two years I have been able to pick these beautiful

flowers to decorate the table. Without you being just the way you are, there would not be this beauty to grace the house."

Moral: Each of us has our own unique flaws. We're all cracked pots. But it's the cracks and flaws we each have that make our lives together so very interesting and rewarding. You've just got to take each person for what they are, and look for the good in them.

Blessed are the flexible, for they shall not be bent out of shape. Remember to appreciate all the different people in your life! Thank you to all the crackpots I know!

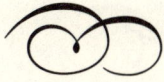

The Sculptor

Early in the last century, sculptor Gutzon Borglum (1867-1941) gazed at the cliffs of South Dakota's Black Hills. He envisioned what no one else could — the sculpted faces of U.S. presidents George Washington, Thomas Jefferson, Abraham Lincoln and Theodore Roosevelt.

Borglum and his crew were suspended on ropes 500 feet above the valley floor. They used everything from chisels to dynamite to create the 5-storey-high visages. It took 14 years to complete the project.

Borglum's housekeeper occasionally went to visit the site. She once asked a worker, "How did Mr. Borglum know that Mr. Lincoln was in that rock?"

How indeed? Borglum knew what was in the rock because he saw with his artist's eye what he could create out of the raw material with which he had to work.

And so it is with us. We are, in fact, the architects of our own lives.

Emerson once said, "What lies before us and what lies ahead of us pales in comparison to what lies within us."

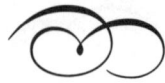

To Be A Kid Again

I want to be a kid again. I want to go back to the time when:
- Decisions were made by going "eeny-meeny-miney-mo."
- Mistakes were corrected by simply exclaiming, "Do over!"
- "Race issue" meant arguing about who ran the fastest.
- Money issues were handled by whoever was the banker in "Monopoly."
- Catching the fireflies could happily occupy an entire evening.
- It wasn't odd to have two or three "best" friends.
- Being old referred to anyone over 20.
- The net on a tennis court was the perfect height to play volleyball and rules didn't matter.
- The worst thing you could catch from the opposite sex was cooties.
- It was magic when Dad would "remove" his thumb.
- It was unbelievable that dodgeball wasn't an Olympic event.
- Having a weapon in school meant being caught with a slingshot.
- Nobody was prettier than Mom was.
- Scrapes and bruises were kissed and made better.
- It was a big deal to finally be tall enough to ride the "big people" rides at the amusement park.
- Getting a foot of snow was a dream come true.
- Abilities were discovered because of a "double-dog-dare."

- Saturday morning cartoons weren't 30-minute ads for action figures.
- No shopping trip was complete unless a new toy was brought home.
- "Oly-oly-oxen-free" made perfect sense.
- Spinning around, getting dizzy and falling down was cause for giggles.
- The worst embarrassment was being picked last for a team.
- Water balloons were the ultimate weapons.
- Baseball cards in the spokes transformed any bike into a motorcycle.
- Taking drugs meant orange-flavoured chewable aspirin.
- Ice cream was considered a basic food group.
- Older siblings were the worst tormentors but also the fiercest protectors.
- War was a card game.
    — *submitted by Sabrina Del Monte, Public Affairs Manager, Canada Safeway*

The Importance of Family

This past weekend my family and I were finally clearing my Mum and Dad's house in New Westminster. This is the house where I grew up after we came to Canada when I was 12 years old.

It is a painful duty to tidy up your parents' "treasures" some five years after their passing. Amongst the thousands of photos, notes, clippings, and bits and pieces of memorabilia I found this newspaper clipping:

It was Grandfather's birthday. He was 79. He got up early, shaved, showered, combed his hair and put on his Sunday best so he would look nice when they came.

He skipped his daily walk to the town café where he had coffee with his cronies. He wanted to be home when they came.

He put his porch chair on the sidewalk so he could get a better view of the street when they drove up to help celebrate his birthday.

At noon, he got tired but decided to forgo his nap so he could be there when they came. Most of the rest of the afternoon he spent near the telephone so he could answer it when they called.

He has five married children, 13 grandchildren and three great-grandchildren.

One son and a daughter live within 10 miles of his place.

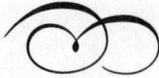

They hadn't visited him for a long time. But today was his birthday and they were sure to come.

At suppertime, he left the cake untouched so they could cut it and have dessert with him. After supper, he sat on the porch waiting.

At 8:30 he went to his room to prepare for bed.

Before retiring, he left a note on the door that read, "Be sure to wake me up when they come."

It was Grandfather's birthday. He was 79.

I hope I never missed a birthday of my Mum and Dad or any other special occasion, but I suppose I did. After a tear or two I made a resolution never to let the contents of this note happen to my wife or children.

It is a sobering thought on the importance of family and special occasions.

— Peter Legge

I've learned...

I've learned.... That the best classroom in the world is at the feet of an elderly person.
I've learned.... That when you're in love, it shows.
I've learned.... That just one person saying to me, "You've made my day!" makes my day.
I've learned.... That having a child fall asleep in your arms is one of the most peaceful feelings in the world.
I've learned.... That being kind is more important than being right.
I've learned.... That you should never say no to a gift from a child.
I've learned.... That I can always pray for someone when I don't have the strength to help him in some other way.
I've learned.... That no matter how serious your life requires you to be, everyone needs a friend to act goofy with.
I've learned.... That sometimes all a person needs is a hand to hold and a heart to understand.
I've learned.... That simple walks with my father around the block on summer nights when I was a child did wonders for me as an adult.
I've learned.... That life is like a roll of toilet paper. The closer it gets to the end, the faster it goes.
I've learned.... That we should be glad God doesn't give us everything we ask for.
I've learned.... That money doesn't buy class.

I've learned.... That it's those small daily happenings that make life so spectacular.
I've learned.... That under everyone's hard shell is someone who wants to be appreciated and loved.
I've learned.... That the Lord didn't do it all in one day. What makes me think I can?
I've learned.... That to ignore the facts does not change the facts.
I've learned.... That when you plan to get even with someone, you are only letting that person continue to hurt you.
I've learned.... That love, not time, heals all wounds.
I've learned.... That the easiest way for me to grow as a person is to surround myself with people smarter than I am.
I've learned.... That everyone you meet deserves to be greeted with a smile.
I've learned.... That there's nothing sweeter than sleeping with your babies and feeling their breath on your cheeks.
I've learned.... That no one is perfect until you fall in love with them.
I've learned.... That life is tough, but I'm tougher.
I've learned.... That opportunities are never lost; someone will take the ones you miss.
I've learned.... That when you harbor bitterness, happiness will dock elsewhere.

I've learned.... That I wish I could have told my Dad that I love him one more time before he passed away.

I've learned.... That one should keep his words both soft and tender, because tomorrow he may have to eat them.

I've learned.... That a smile is an inexpensive way to improve your looks.

I've learned.... That I can't choose how I feel, but I can choose what I do about it.

I've learned.... That when your newly born grandchild holds your little finger in his little fist, that you're hooked for life.

I've learned.... That everyone wants to live on top of the mountain, but all the happiness and growth occurs while you're climbing it.

I've learned.... ... That it is best to give advice in only two circumstances; when it is requested and when it is a life-threatening situation.

I've learned.... That the less time I have to work with, the more things I get done.

— *Andy Rooney*

5 Tips to Gaining Information About Your Competitors

In war, the army who acquires more knowledge and understanding of their enemy's strengths and weaknesses and how to react to them increases their chances of winning the battle.

Salespeople with good information about their competitors, strengths and weaknesses increase their chances of winning the economic war. They know how to position their products, services and themselves so they are perceived as having superior quality and value.

1. **Who are your competitors?** Have a file of your competitors' literature, brochures, strengths and weaknesses (i.e. sales and marketing strategies, unique products or services, etc.).
2. **Who are the salespeople I am competing with on each account?** What are their names, strengths and weaknesses?
3. **What are the situations or applications in which the competition's products or services have a distinct advantage?**
4. **What is the competition's marketing strategy?**

Understand what successful marketing strategies your competitors are using to attract new clients.
5. **Gain information about your competitors when you lose deals.** Send a letter to a customer after losing a deal thanking them for the opportunity to bid on the project. Tell them your manager will be calling them to get some constructive feedback for improvement.

"There is no security in this life, only opportunity."
— *Douglas MacArthur*

— *submitted by Joe McCracken*
Royal Bank of Canada

The Chinese Bamboo

Leonardo da Vinci painted the Mona Lisa when he was 50 years old. Clara Barton founded the American Red Cross when she was 59. George Bernard Shaw wrote his famous drama, *Saint Joan,* when he was 67. Cervantes completed *Don Quixote* when he was almost 70. Mary Baker Eddy founded an international daily newspaper, *The Christian Science Monitor,* at age 86. Will Durant sold a series of television programs when he was in his nineties. And who knows, maybe you'll complete your greatest achievement when you're 100.

Some people resemble desert grass in springtime; they flourish overnight. For example, Mozart composed his first symphony when he was eight years old. But others — and perhaps you or someone you know belongs to this group — require many years of preparation before they tap their potential. These people resemble the moso — a Chinese bamboo plant.

When a farmer plants a moso, he can take care of it for an entire year — watering, weeding and fertilizing — and not see any signs of growth. He can continue pampering his moso for another year and still not see any growth. It can go on like this for up to FIVE YEARS, after which time the moso will finally burst through the soil and within six weeks become a towering 90-foot Chinese bamboo plant! That's the height of a nine-storey office building!

All those years when the farmer saw no growth above the ground, the moso was spreading its root system — miles of roots — getting ready! And that's the way many people are. They need lots of time to get ready!

Perhaps you've been frustrated with yourself for not improving as quickly as you'd like to — for not getting that promotion, or breaking 90 on the golf course. Perhaps you've been frustrated with your spouse, your son or daughter, an associate at work, or a friend, for not improving as fast as he or she appeared capable of. But have patience. Spreading roots and clearing one's thoughts of debilitating fears and doubts might take a while. But eventually there will be improvement. When it occurs, it could be as sudden and visible as the growth of the Chinese bamboo!

— *From* The Unlimited Times
Joel H. Weldon & Assoc. Inc.

Love, Wealth & Success

A woman came out of her house and saw three old men with long white beards sitting in her front yard. She did not recognize them. She said, "I don't think I know you, but you must be hungry. Please come in and have something to eat."

"Is the man of the house home?" they asked. "No," she replied. "He's out." "Then we cannot come in," they replied.

In the evening when her husband came home, she told him what had happened. "Go tell them I am home and invite them in!"

The woman went out and invited the men in. "We do not go into a house together," they replied. "Why is that?" she asked. One of the old men explained: "His name is Wealth," he said pointing to one of his friends, and pointing to another one said, "He is Success and I am Love." Then he added, "Now go in and discuss with your husband which one of us you want in your home." The woman went in and told her husband what was said. Her husband was overjoyed. "How nice!" he said. "Since that is the case, let us invite Wealth. Let him come and fill our home with wealth!" His wife disagreed. "My dear, why don't we invite Success?"

Their daughter-in-law was listening from the other corner of the house. She jumped in with her own suggestion: "Would it not be better to invite Love? Our home will then be filled with love!" "Let us heed our daughter-in-law's advice," said the husband to his wife. "Go out and invite

Love to be our guest."

The woman went out and asked the three old men, "Which one of you is Love? Please come in and be our guest." Love got up and started walking towards the house. The other two also got up and followed him. Surprised, the lady asked Wealth and Success, "I only invited Love. Why are you coming in?"

The old men replied together, "If you had invited Wealth or Success, the other two of us would have stayed out but since you invited Love, where he goes, we go with him. Wherever there is Love, there is also Wealth and Success!"

The Small Stuff

A philosophy professor stood before his class with some items in front of him. When class began, wordlessly he picked up a large empty mayonnaise jar and proceeded to fill it with rocks, rocks about 2 inches in diameter. He then asked the students if the jar was full. They agreed that it was.

So the professor then picked up a box of pebbles and poured them into the jar. He shook the jar lightly. The pebbles, of course, rolled into the open areas between the rocks. He then asked the students again if the jar was full. They agreed it was.

The professor picked up a box of sand and poured it into the jar. Of course, the sand filled up everything else. "Now," said the professor, "I want you to recognize that this is your life. The rocks are important things — your family, your partner, your health and your children — anything that is so important to you that if it were lost, you would be nearly destroyed. The pebbles are the other things that matter like your job, your house and your car. The sand is everything else. The small stuff.

"If you put the sand into the jar first, there is no room for the pebbles or the rocks. The same goes for your life. If you spend all your energy and time on the small stuff, you will never have room for the things that are important to you. Pay attention to the things that are critical to your happiness. Play with your children. Take time to get medical

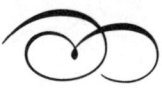

check-ups. Take your partner out dancing. Spend quality time with your friends and family. There will always be time to go to work, clean the house, give a dinner party and fix the disposal. Take care of the rocks first — the things that really matter. Set your priorities. The rest is just sand."

English is a Crazy Language

Let's face it — English is a crazy language. There is neither egg in eggplant, ham in hamburger nor pine in pineapple. English muffins weren't invented in England or French fries in France. Sweetmeats are candies while sweetbreads, which aren't sweet, are meat.

We take English for granted. But if we explore its paradoxes, we find that quicksand can work slowly, boxing rings are square and a guinea pig is neither from Guinea nor is it a pig.

And why is it that writers write but fingers don't fing, grocers don't groce and hammers don't ham? If the plural of tooth is teeth, why isn't the plural of booth, beeth? One goose, 2 geese — so one moose, 2 meese? One index, 2 indices?

Doesn't it seem crazy that you can make amends but not one amend that you comb through annals of history but not a single annal? If you have a bunch of odds and ends and get rid of all but one of them, what do you call it?

If teachers taught, why don't preachers praught? If vegetarians eat vegetables, what does a humanitarian eat? If you wrote a letter, perhaps you bote your tongue?

Sometimes I think all the English speakers should be committed to an asylum for the verbally insane. In what language do people recite at a play and play at a recital? Ship by truck and send cargo by ship? Have noses that run and

feet that smell? Park on driveways and drive on parkways?

How can a slim chance and a fat chance be the same, while a wise man and a wise guy are opposites? How can overlook and oversee be opposite, while quite a few and quite a lot are alike? How can the weather be hot as hell one day and cold as hell the other day?

Have you noticed that we talk about certain things only when they are absent? Have you ever seen a horseful carriage or a strapful gown? Met a sung hero or experience requited love? Have you ever run into someone who was combobulated, gruntled, ruly or picable? And where are all those people who ARE spring chickens or who would ACTUALLY hurt a fly?

You have to marvel at the unique lunacy of a language in which your house can burn up as it burns down, in which you fill in a form by filling it out and in which an alarm clock goes off by going on.

People, not computers invented English, and it reflects the creativity of the human race (which, of course, isn't a race at all). That is why, when the stars are out, they are visible, but when the lights are out, they are invisible. And why, when I wind up my watch, I start it, but when I wind up this essay, I end it.

The Seven Wonders

A group of geography students studied the Seven Wonders of the World. At the end of that section, the students were asked to list what they considered to be the Seven Wonders of the World. Though there was some disagreement, the following got the most votes:

1. Egypt's Great Pyramids
2. Taj Mahal
3. Eiffel Tower
4. Panama Canal
5. Empire State Building
6. St. Peter's Basilica
7. China's Great Wall

While gathering the votes, the teacher noted that one student, a quiet girl, hadn't turned in her paper yet. So she asked the girl if she was having trouble with her list. The quiet girl replied, "Yes, a little. I couldn't quite make up my mind because there were so many." The teacher said, "Well, tell us what you have, and maybe we can help." The girl hesitated, then read, "I think the Seven Wonders of the World are:

1. To Touch
2. To Taste

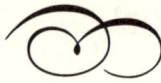

3. To See
4. To Hear"

She hesitated a little, "And then

5. To Run
6. To Laugh
7. To Love"

It is far too easy for us to look at the exploits of man and refer to them as "wonders" while we overlook all God has done, regarding them as merely "ordinary." May you be reminded today of those things that are truly wondrous.

Think It Over

Today we have higher buildings and wider highways,
But shorter temperaments and narrower points of view.

We spend more, but enjoy less
We have bigger houses, but smaller families
We have more compromises, but less time
We have more knowledge, but less judgement
We have more medicines, but less health.

We have multiplied our possessions, but reduced our values
We talk much, we love only a little, and we hate too much.

We have reached the moon and come back, but we find it troublesome to cross our own street and meet our neighbours.
We have conquered the outer space, but not our inner space.

We have higher incomes, but fewer morals . . .
These are times with more liberty, but less joy . . .
With much more food, but less nutrition . . .

These are days in which two salaries get home, but divorces increase.
These are times of finer houses, but more broken homes.

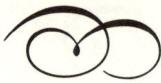

That's why I propose that from today:

Do not keep anything for a special occasion, because every day you live is a special occasion.
Search for knowledge, read more, sit on your front porch and admire the view without paying attention to the needs.
Pass more time with your family, eat your favourite food, and visit the place you love.
Life is a chain of moments of enjoyment; it isn't only survival.
Use your crystal goblets. Do not save your best perfume, use it every time you feel you want it.
Take out from your vocabulary phrases like "One of these days" and "some day."
Let's write that letter we thought of writing "One of these days."
Let's tell our families and friends how much we love them.
Do not delay anything that adds laughter and joy to your life.
Every day, hour and minute are special . . .
And you don't know if it will be your last . . .

The Voice of Experience

The newest thing about the new economy? The notion of tough times and economic failure. It's something that many business leaders have either forgotten about or never experienced.

What's the best strategy for making it through a bad patch?

Warren Bennis, distinguished Professor of Business Administration, Founding Chairman of the Leadership Institute, Marshall School of Business, University of Southern California, says the following:

I have been alive for 76 years, and I think this is a damn good time to be on this earth. The Internet Age has presented us with a marvelous opportunity: We're starting out fresh, having to learn the ropes together. What we're seeing now are little setbacks. And if there's one thing that the older generation understands well, it's that there are things called "cycles." And cycles teach you patience.

I don't want to make it sound easy, because it can be heartbreaking to have to fire people. Nevertheless running a business today is as terrific an education as a young person can get. In a bumpy economy, you learn quickly to make courageous choices.

If you're a leader, probably the biggest mistake you can make during any kind of downturn is to choke up.

Remember the Flying Wallendas? Karl, the patriarch of the Wallenda family, fell 120 feet to his death while trying to walk a tightwire between two office buildings. Later, his wife said that before the stunt, Karl had seemed concerned about falling. He fell because he was focused on not falling, rather than on getting to the other side.

In tough times, remember Karl Wallenda. When you concentrate on not losing, rather than on winning, you'll find yourself dead on the ground.

How to Beat a Bad Mood

With a little effort, you can put it behind you

Are you having one of those days — or weeks — when every little thing seems to annoy you? Are you wondering if your little black cloud will ever disperse, letting you back in the sunshine again? Even if you do nothing about it, your grouchiness will probably pass eventually with time, but with a little effort you can put it behind you much faster.

1. Stop and LISTEN to what's on your mind. Be your own best friend and give yourself an empathetic ear. What exactly is it that's bothering you? What are you feeling? Disappointment? Resentment? Jealousy? You'll be amazed how much better you feel just by this simple process of unburdening yourself, TO yourself!
2. Take a hike! That's right, a brisk walk can do wonders towards lifting your spirits, raising your energy level, and clearing your mind of those dark clouds, even opening the way to creative solutions to some of those worrisome problems.
3. Give yourself a pep talk. Here again, being your own best friend is the key. What would your "ideal" friend say to you if he or she wanted to give you a morale boost? Okay, you say it to your self! There, that wasn't so hard, and to your subconscious mind, it feels just as

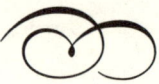

good, whether you say it or someone else does!
4. Refocus on your goals. Remind yourself of the direction you want to be heading. Don't let anything distract, deter or derail you from your priorities. Zoom in on them and let your laser focus cut through your gloomy thoughts and recharge your mental batteries.
5. Remember to laugh at yourself. If you don't, everyone else will! So don't take yourself seriously, just take what you DO very seriously. Think of it this way, the size of your funeral will be determined by . . . the weather! That's right! If you live in North Dakota and die in January, you're out there all alone! No one's coming! So keep your sense of humour always.

Instructions for Life

1. Take into account that great love and great achievements involve great risk.
2. When you lose, don't lose the lesson.
3. Follow the three R's:
   Respect for Self
   Respect for Others
   Responsibility for all your actions.
4. Remember that not getting what you want is sometimes a wonderful stroke of luck.
5. Learn the rules so you know how to break them properly.
6. Don't let a little dispute injure a great friendship.
7. When you realize you've made a mistake, take immediate steps to correct it.
8. Spend some time alone every day.
9. Open your arms to change but don't let go of your values.
10. Remember that silence is sometimes the best answer.
11. Live a good, honourable life. Then when you get older and think back, you'll be able to enjoy it a second time.
12. A loving atmosphere in your home is the foundation for your life.
13. In disagreements with loved ones, deal only with the current situation. Don't bring up the past.
14. Share your knowledge. It's a way to achieve immortality.
15. Be gentle with the earth.

16. Once a year, go someplace you've never been before.
17. Remember that the best relationship is one in which your love for each other exceeds your need for each other.
18. Judge your success by what you had to give up in order to get it.
19. Approach love and cooking with reckless abandon.

"The Strangest Secret"

At the end of this paragraph is a statement which can change your life. Don't read it yet! It deserves an explanation first. It's about growing as a person and learning. When many people first encounter this statement, they are stunned that it is never mentioned during their years of high school or university education. This statement isn't the key to everything, but if put to use, it can certainly help you become an even more effective, capable person than you are right now. Here it is: "You become what you think about most of the time."

The late Earl Nightingale made that statement many years ago. He called it "The Strangest Secret." More recently his theory was proven to be fact. Researchers studying the human memory process have discovered that most of what you know was learned through repetition.

For example, anything you read or hear just once will be 66 per cent forgotten within 24 hours. Yet, whatever you read or hear several times a day for just one week is virtually memorized at the end of that week! This means that by reading or listening to something over and over again, it becomes a habit of thought. Through repetition it becomes part of you!

So what are you thinking about, and what are you becoming? Answer that question in terms of just one segment of your life: the time you spend driving your car.

You may be surprised to learn that you probably spend over 400 hours a year sitting in your automobile! This is time when your hands and your eyes are busy but your mind isn't. It's the ideal time in which to feed your mind with whatever you want to become. And the best way to do that is to turn off the radio and listen to an audiocassette or CD.

A Whisper or a Brick

A young and successful executive was travelling down a neighbourhood street, going a bit too fast in his new Jaguar. He was watching for kids darting out from between cars and saw something. As his car passed, no children appeared. Instead, a brick smashed into the Jag's side door! He slammed on the brakes and spun the Jag back to the spot from where the brick had been thrown. He jumped out of the car, grabbed some kid and pushed him up against a parked car shouting, "What was that all about and who are you? Just what the hell are you doing? That's a new car and that brick you threw is going to cost a lot of money. Why did you do that?"

"Please, mister please. I'm sorry, I didn't know what else to do," pleaded the youngster. "I threw the brick because no one else would stop . . ."

Tears were dripping down the boy's chin as he pointed around the parked car. "It's my brother," he said. "He rolled off the curb and fell out of his wheelchair and I can't lift him up." Sobbing, the boy asked the executive, "Would you please help me get him back into his wheelchair? He's hurt and he's too heavy for me."

Moved beyond words, the driver tried to swallow the rapidly swelling lump in his throat. He lifted the young man back into the wheelchair and took out his handkerchief and wiped the scrapes and cuts, checking to see that everything

was going to be okay.

"Thank you and God bless you," the grateful child said. The man then watched the little boy push his brother down the sidewalk toward their home. It was a long walk back to his Jaguar — a long, slow walk.

He kept the dent to remind himself not to go through life so fast that someone has to throw a brick at you to get your attention. God whispers in your soul and speaks to your heart. Sometimes when you don't have time to listen, He has to throw a "brick" at you.

It's your choice: Listen to the Whisper or wait for the Brick.

Organize Your Life

The Top Eight Organizational Tips to Increase Your Effectiveness

1. Never Touch the Same Piece of Paper Twice. File it, trash it or act on it.
2. Never Use the Phone When You Can Use E-Mail. It's faster, easier, more efficient, and automatically documents your communications.
3. Schedule Meetings Seven Minutes Apart. When someone knows they've only got seven minutes, they get right to the point.
4. Don't Intermingle Tasks. Group similar activities together and do them all at once.
5. Invest in the Tools Needed to Get Your Job Done Efficiently. In the long run, it's cheaper to buy what you need to improve production rather than make do with outdated or ineffective equipment.
6. Listen to Teaching Tapes in the Car. Instead of being stressed out by traffic, you can engage your brain. Learn another language; improve your sales, business and management skills; and master the latest strategies for success by listening to tapes during drive time.
7. Eliminate Needless Interruptions. Create a block of uninterrupted work time by closing your office door. Let your secretary, voice mail or answering machine record your messages — then return calls later.

8. When In Doubt, Throw It Out! If you wonder if you'll ever need it, trust me, you won't.

— *Peter Lowe*

15 Things That Take A Lifetime To Learn

1. Never under any circumstances take a sleeping pill and a laxative on the same night.
2. If you had to identify, in one word, the reason why the human race has not achieved, and never will achieve, its full potential, that word would be "meetings."
3. And when God, who created the entire universe with all of its glories, decides to deliver a message to humanity, He will not use, as His messenger, a person on cable TV with a bad hairstyle.
4. You should not confuse your career with your life.
5. When trouble arises and things look bad, there is always one individual who perceives a solution and is willing to take command. Very often, that individual is crazy.
6. Nobody cares if you can't dance well. Just get up and dance.
7. Never lick a steak knife.
8. The most powerful force in the universe is gossip.
9. You will never find anybody who can give you a clear and compelling reason why we observe daylight savings time.
10. You should never say anything to a woman that even remotely suggests that you think she's pregnant unless you can see an actual baby emerging from her at that moment.
11. There comes a time when you should stop expecting other people to make a big deal about your birthday.

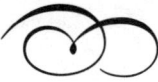

      That time is age 11.
12. The one thing that unites all human beings, regardless of age, gender, religion, economic status or ethnic background, is that, deep down inside, we all believe that we are above average drivers.
13. A person, who is nice to you, but rude to the waiter, is not a nice person.
14. Your friends love you anyway.
15. Never argue with an idiot — people watching can't tell which is which.

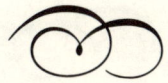

Service

In the summer of 2002, my family and I cruised to Alaska on the Sea Princess. It was seven wonderful family days, Vancouver to Skagway, Sitka and Juneau and back to Vancouver.

While in Skagway we took the White Pass and Yukon Railway train ride to the summit. The journey is only 20 miles but does climb 2,865 feet and is considered one of the steepest railroad grades in North America. In fact, it is among only 36 engineering feats in the world to have been declared an historic civil engineering landmark.

This 20-mile journey traces the footsteps of 100,000 hopefuls who came to Alaska searching for gold in the famous gold rush of 1898.

Here is the dramatic ending – of the 100,000 who headed north to Alaska only 30,000 to 40,000 actually reached the gold fields near Dawson. Of those only 20,000 bothered to look for gold. Four thousand or so prospectors found gold and less than 100 of those became rich. Only a handful of those were able to keep their newfound wealth from slipping through their fingers.

Who really became wealthy? It was those who provided a SERVICE for others; the essentials for living life in Alaska in 1898! More than 100 years later, it is still those providing a service for others, who are successful over the long haul.

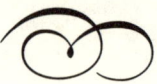

How do you provide quality service to your clients, suppliers or fellow workers?
Remember he who excels in SERVICE really can strike gold.

—*Peter Legge*

Secrets to Success

1. How you think is everything. Always be positive. Think success, not failure. Beware of a negative environment.
2. Decide upon your true dreams and goals. Write down your specific goals and develop a plan to reach them.
3. Take action. Goals are nothing without action. Don't be afraid to get started. Just do it.
4. Never stop learning. Go back to school or read books. Get training and acquire skills.
5. Be persistent and work hard. Success is a marathon, not a sprint. Never give up.
6. Learn to analyze details. Get all the facts, all the input. Learn from your mistakes.
7. Focus your time and money. Don't let other people or things distract you.
8. Don't be afraid to innovate. Be different. Following the herd is a sure way to mediocrity.
9. Deal and communicate with people effectively. No person is an island. Learn to understand and motivate others.
10. Be honest and dependable. Take responsibility. Otherwise Numbers 1-9 won't matter.

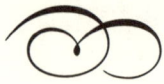

I've Learned . . .

That no matter what happens, or how bad it seems today, life does go on and it will be better tomorrow.

That you can tell a lot about a person by the way he/she handles these three things — a rainy day, lost luggage and tangled Christmas tree lights.

That regardless of your relationship with your parents, you'll miss them when they're gone from your life.

That making a "living" is not the same thing as making a "life."

That life sometimes gives you a second chance.

That you shouldn't go through life with a catcher's mitt on both hands. You need to be able to throw something back.

That if you pursue happiness, it will elude you. But if you focus on your family, your friends, the needs of others, your work and doing the very best you can, happiness will find you.

That whenever I decide something with an open heart, I usually make the right decision.

That even when I have pains, I don't have to be one.

That every day you should reach out and touch someone. People love that human touch — holding hands, a warm hug or just a friendly pat on the back.

That I still have a lot to learn.

Make It A Habit

Make it a habit to treat each day as a gift.
After all, each day happens only once and lasts only 24
 hours.

Make it a habit to treat people with respect.
You will be amazed how fast respect is returned with love.

Make it a habit to tell people how you feel about them.
If you don't, they simply will never know.

Make it a habit to deliver more than you promise.
It's okay to risk being counted on.

Make it a habit to serve others.
The act of service has no prerequisites.

Make it a habit to follow your conscience.
Your inner voice speaks quietly . . .
Be prepared to stop talking long enough to listen.

Make it a habit to learn something new every day.
Recognize that when the student is ready, the teacher will
 appear.

Make it a habit to reflect and renew.

The fact that seasons change is one of nature's many
   lessons.

Make it a habit to follow your dreams.
If you don't chase your dream, no one else will do it for you.

Make it a habit to see the best in others.
Would you not want others to look for the best in you?

Make it a habit to be thankful for your blessings.
There are thankful people who have far less than you or I.

Make it a habit to put people before things.
"Things" will not miss you when you're gone.

And lastly, Make it a habit to make it a great day.
For if you practice this habit long enough . . . you will make
   it a great life.

              — *Peter van Dongen*

The Echo of Life

A man and his son were walking in the forest. Suddenly the boy trips and feeling a sharp pain he screams, "Ahhhhhh!"

Surprised, he hears a voice coming from the mountain, "Ahhhhhh!"

Filled with curiosity, he screams: "Who are you?" but the only answer he receives is: "Who are you?"

This makes him angry, so he screams: "You are a coward!" and the voice answers: "You are a coward!" He looks at his father, asking, "Dad, what is going on?"

"Son," the man replies, "pay attention!" Then he screams, "I admire you!"

The voice answers, "I admire you!"

The father shouts, "You are wonderful!" and the voice answers: "You are wonderful!"

The boy is surprised, but still can't understand what is going on.

Then the father explains, "People call this ECHO, but truly it is LIFE! Life always gives you back what you give out! Life is a mirror of actions. If you want more love, give more love! If you want more kindness, give more kindness! If you want understanding and respect, give understanding and respect! If you want people to be patient and respectful to you, give patience and respect! This rule of nature applies to every aspect of our lives."

Life always gives you back what you give out. Your life is

not a coincidence, but a mirror of your own doings.
— *Author Unknown*

The Plumber

I hired a plumber to help me restore an old farmhouse, and after he had just finished a rough first day on the job, a flat tire made him lose an hour of work and his electric drill quit, his ancient one-ton truck refused to start. As I drove him home, he sat in stony silence.

On arriving he invited me in to meet his family. As we walked toward the front door, he paused briefly at a small tree, touching the tips of the branches with both hands. Upon opening the door he had undergone an amazing transformation. His tanned face was wreathed in smiles and he hugged his two small children and gave his wife a kiss.

Afterward he walked me to the car. We passed the tree and my curiosity got the better of me. I asked him about what I had seen him do at the little tree.

"Oh, that's my trouble tree," he replied. "I know I can't help having troubles on the job, but one thing's for sure, those troubles don't belong in the house with my wife and the children. So I just hang them up on the tree every night when I come home and ask God to take care of them. Then in the morning I pick them up again. Funny thing is," he smiled, "when I come out in the morning to pick them up, there aren't nearly as many as I remember hanging up the night before."

If Only

If Only 'tis a human cry
When everything is lost
And nothing else from fate is left
Upon the fire to toss.

If Only I'd done this or that
If Only come or gone
If Only taken up the cross
If Only sung that song.

If Only they are little words
Which each of us have said
And will so many times again
Before we all are dead.

– Yvonne Covey-Boyd
St. John Ambulance

Keeping on — anyway

It's part of the business world when we encounter frustrations, obstacles and obstructions. Then what? Then it's time to hang onto one powerful, positive word — endure!

To endure means: "Inch by inch, anything is a cinch."

To endure means: "There is no gain without pain."

To endure means: "When faced with a mountain, I will not quit. I will keep on striving until I climb over, find a pass through, tunnel underneath . . . or simply stay and turn the mountain into a gold mine."

To endure means: "I have to look at what I have, not at what I've lost."

So you are unemployed? To endure means you're going to keep on living a meaningful life anyway.

So you have people problems and are frustrated with regulations and roadblocks and negative forces? You are so tired of fighting you'd like to throw in the towel and quit?

What does it mean to endure? It means to remember that when you face problems, you keep this point in the forefront of your mind: people, problems and pressures are constantly changing, so don't split. You'll run into the same basic frustrations no matter where you go.

To endure means you keep on being positive about life — anyway!

Never forget this wise warning:

Never make a negative decision in a down time.
This is only a phase that you are going through. It will pass. When it is over, you'll be glad you hung in there!

Take Time To Think

Throughout the Universe there is order in the movement of planets, in nature and in the functioning of the human mind. A mind that is in its natural state of order is in harmony with the universe and such a mind is timeless.

Your life is an expression of your mind. You are the creator of your own universe for as a human being you are free to will whatever state of being you desire through the use of your thoughts and words, there is great power there. It can be a blessing or a curse; it's entirely up to you. For the quality of your life is brought about by the quality of your thinking, think about that.

Thoughts produce actions. Look at what you are thinking now. See the pettiness and the envy and the greed and the fear and all the other attitudes that cause you pain and discomfort. Realize the one thing you have absolute control over is your attitude.

See the effect it has on those around you. For each life is linked to all life and your words carry chain reactions, like a stone thrown into a pond. If your thinking is in order your words will flow directly from the heart, creating ripples of love.

Your future depends on many things, but mostly on you.
— Frank Tyger, Author

If you truly want to change your world my friends, you must change your thinking. Reason is your greatest tool; it

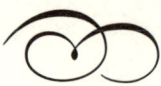

creates an atmosphere of understanding, which leads to caring, which is love. Choose your words with care and always Take Time To Think.

— *From* The Hospitality Jungle, *Max Hitchins*

Excuses For Not Taking Action

1. We tried that before.
2. This place is different.
3. It costs too much.
4. That's beyond our responsibility.
5. We're all too busy to do that.
6. That's not my job.
7. It's too radical a change.
8. We don't have the time.
9. Not enough help.
10. Our place is too small for it.
11. Not practical for operating people.
12. The men will never buy it.
13. The union will scream.
14. We've never done it before.
15. It's against regulations.
16. Runs up overhead.
17. We don't have the authority.
18. That's too ivory tower.
19. Let's get back to reality.
20. That's not our problem.
21. If it ain't broke, don't fix it.
22. You're right — but . . .
23. You're two years ahead of your time.
24. We don't have the personnel.

25. It isn't in the budget.
26. Good thought, but impractical.
27. Let's give it more thought.
28. Top management would never go for it.
29. Let's put it in writing.
30. We'd lose money in the long run.
31. It's never been tried before.
32. Let's shelve it for the time being.
33. Let's form a committee.
34. Has anyone else ever tried it?
35. Let's put it on the back burner.
36. That won't work in my department.
37. The Executive Committee will never . . .
38. Let's look into that further before we act.
39. Let's all sleep on it.
40. I know someone who tried that.
41. We've always done it this way.
42. It's hopelessly complex.
43. I wasn't in the loop.

Forget excuses — think of what you CAN do.

Reality

Controlling your emotions increases your control over the situation.

There may not be much you can do about how things are changing in the organization. But there is a lot you can do about how you react to the situation. You have total control over that.

Nobody else is in charge of your attitude. So, if your attitude is upbeat and positive, you get all the credit. On the other hand, if you're reacting negatively to the changes, that's a choice you have made. And you have to pay the consequences.

It won't do you or the company any good if you go around upset about things. You waste too much mental and physical energy going to work with a bad attitude every day. It poisons your job satisfaction, clouds your judgment and probably hurts your chances for success in the future.

Anger, frustration or resentment offer no benefits. Might as well get over it.

"Never become irritable waiting for things to get better. If you'll be patient, you'll find that you can wait much faster."

— *Unknown*

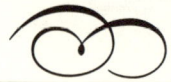

The Leadership Skills of Elizabeth I

1. Ask yourself who would I be without my job? The answer may give you a sense of your own strength or may warn you of your vulnerability.
2. Value your word as the word of a Prince. Too many business leaders today look upon honour and honesty as excess baggage or as unaffordable luxuries — stuff that gets in the way of real business.
3. Tolerance and generosity are typically the marks of an effective leader.
4. Whenever possible deal with issues not people. In conflict or extreme instances calling for reprimand, avoid making it personal.
5. Actions speak louder. As I get older I pay less attention to what men and women say but more attention to what they do.
6. No leader is a solo act. We are indeed a diverse team of talented individuals.
7. Know who is who and who to know. Elizabeth I made it her business to know everyone of talent and influence in her realm. She forged personal relationships with movers and shakers drawing conclusions about what they could do for her and against her. An Old Italian proverb says — "Know your friends but stay closer to your enemies."

8. Trust but verify.
9. An effective leader learns the language of those he or she leads. Learn the language that speaks of dollars, value, time, rewards and risks. This is what business is made up of.
10. Make expectations clear and lofty.

— *Alan Axelrod,* Elizabeth I CEO: Strategic Lessons from the Leader Who Built An Empire

Count Your Blessings

If you woke up this morning with more health than illness, you are more blessed than the million who will not survive this week.

If you have never experienced the danger of battle, the loneliness of imprisonment, the agony of torture, or the pangs of starvation, you are ahead of 500 million people in the world.

If you can attend a church meeting without fear of harassment, arrest, torture or death, you are more blessed than 3 billion people in the world.

If you have food in the refrigerator, clothes on your back, a roof overhead and a place to sleep, you are richer than 75% of this world.

If you have money in the bank, in your wallet, and spare change in a dish someplace, you are among the top 8% of the world's wealthy.

If your parents are still alive and still married, you are very rare.

If you hold up your head with a smile on your face and are truly thankful, you are blessed because the majority can, but most do not.

If you can hold someone's hand, hug them or even touch them on the shoulder, you are blessed because you can offer a healing touch.

If you can read this message, you just received a double

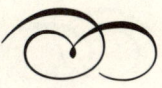

blessing in that someone was thinking of you, and furthermore, you are more blessed than over 2 billion people in the world who cannot read at all.

Count your blessings.

The Winners Are Still Winning

You can prosper, regardless of the current economic situation.

A management psychologist described a conversation he once had with his banker in which he was asked the following question:

"Jim, you get around behind the scenes in a lot of businesses. What do you make of the current economic situation?"

"The winners are still winning!" he answered, and went on to explain that, despite tough times, some people still pursue and achieve their goals. No matter how pessimistic the news may be, the winners continue to wring triumph out of adversity.

A refreshing and encouraging thought, isn t it? What is it that winners do to continue winning? Here are six common characteristics of winners:

1. Winners depend upon themselves above all else. They'll put any advantage they can acquire to work, but they primarily rely on their own talents. The economy and the government may affect business positively or negatively, but the winners know the only constants lie within themselves.
2. The winners also recognize the importance of other

people. They know that human relations are even more crucial during hard times. But because they depend ultimately on themselves, winners don't seek scapegoats among the people they work with. They accept full responsibility for their actions and waste little time blaming.

3. Winners accept and cope realistically with their own faults. They feel no compulsion to live up to the image of "big business executive," no matter how popular that image may be.

4. Winners eagerly listen to and learn from almost anyone, but in the end, they act on their own convictions.

5. The tenacious pursuit of goals is another characteristic of winners. They'll change pace, tactics and priorities, but always with one goal in mind. For them, the goal is fixed; only the strategy changes.

6. And finally, winners care more about an accomplishment than about the ensuing rewards. They love the pursuit, the endeavour itself. Some winners may expect to be paid handsomely for their work, but they still see the work itself as a greater monument to their talents than any amount of money.

—*from* The Unlimited Times
Joel H. Weldon & Assoc.

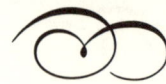

Common Mistakes Salespeople Make

1. They talk too much.
2. They give information before they get information.
3. They fail to observe and integrate early prospect signals.
4. They fail to effectively manage rejection and failure.
5. They sell when they should prospect and prospect when they should be selling.
6. They don't listen and take notes while the prospect is talking.
7. They inject their own values and/or buying prejudices into the sales process.
8. They don't effectively read buyer signals and act accordingly.
9. They sell features and price rather than value and customer benefits.
10. They don't keep good records or evaluate their wins and losses.
11. They don't work as hard to keep the business as they did to get it.
12. They don't ask for the business.
13. They focus on making the sale rather than selling the relationship.
14. They don't invest enough time and money in their self-development.
15. They confuse the importance of knowing with that of caring.

An Interview with God!

I dreamed I had an interview with God. "Come in," God said, "So, you would like to interview Me?" "If you have the time," I said. God smiled and said, "My time is eternity and that is enough time to do everything. What questions do you have in mind to ask me?"

"What surprises you most about mankind?" I asked.

God answered, "That they get bored of being children, are in a rush to grow up and then long to be children again. They lose their health to make money and then lose their money to restore their health. That by thinking anxiously about the future, they forget the present, such that they live neither for the present or the future. They live as if they will never die, and they die as if they had never lived."

God's hands took mine and we were silent for awhile and then I asked, "As a parent, what are some of life's lessons you want your children to learn?"

God replied with a smile, "To learn that they cannot make anyone love them. What they can do is to let themselves be loved. To learn that what is most valuable is not what they have in their lives, but whom they have in their lives. To learn that it is not good to compare themselves to others. All will be judged individually on their own merits, not as a group on a comparison basis! To learn that a rich person is not the one who has the most, but is one who needs the least. To learn that it only takes a few seconds to open

profound wounds in persons we love, and that it takes many years to heal them. To learn to forgive by practicing forgiveness. To learn that there are persons that love them dearly, but simply do not know how to express or show their feelings. To learn that money can buy everything but happiness. To learn that two people can look at the same thing and see it totally different. To learn that a true friend is someone who knows everything about him or her, and likes them anyway. To learn that it is not always enough that they be forgiven by others, but that they have to forgive themselves."

I sat there for awhile enjoying the moment. I thanked Him for his time and for all that He has done for my family and me and He replied, "Anytime. I'm here 24 hours a day. All you have to do is ask for me and I'll answer."

People will forget what you said. People will forget what you did, but people will never forget how you made them feel.

— *Submitted by Karen Atkinson, TV Program Editor,*
TV WEEK Magazine

Forgiveness & Love

One of the most wonderful stories about forgiveness and love started many years ago in the Vietnam War. Journalist Patricia Chisholm recalls the story in *Maclean's* magazine:

Nine-year-old Phan Thi Kim Phuc was fleeing her village when American bombs intended for military installations started exploding all around her. She recalls, "Right away, I know my clothes are burning, everything, and I saw my hand, my arm burning." But then she started to run, desperate to escape the circle of fire. There was, she says, "No more thinking." Just overwhelming fear, and later a searing heat. She had terrible injuries to her back, where great swaths of skin were destroyed by the napalm, a thickener that turns gasoline into a jelly-like concoction that sticks to surfaces, including skin, as it burns. At the scene, photographer Nick Ut rushed her to a nearby hospital, where she stayed for 14 months, enduring many operations. Nick's dramatic photograph, which won him a Pulitzer Prize, captures the agony of the moment.

Now living in Canada after years of rehabilitation and adjustment to Western life, Kim has displayed a remarkable capacity to forgive. In the fall of 1996, she participated in a Veteran's Day ceremony at the Vietnam War Memorial in Washington D.C. There, she had an unanticipated and emotional meeting with Capt. John Plummer, the man who ordered South Vietnamese pilots to make the fateful air

strike on her village. As the two sat side by side, smiling and holding hands, it was clear that Kim bore him nothing but good will. In this respect Kim is rare. Many people would live with resentment and hate that would consume them for years. She has chosen to avoid reflecting on the war. "I never do sorrow like that," she says. "To feel a trace of bitterness, even deep inside, is too tiring, too heavy." Instead, Kim decided to move forward. She is now happily married and has a young son to nurture. Undoubtedly, her ability to love and forgive has accelerated her progress.

— Excerpt from The Power of Focus
Jack Canfield, Mark Victor Hansen, Les Hewitt

Art Linkletter

Art Linkletter is probably best known as an entertainer and show business personality. As a baby, he was abandoned and then adopted by a church minister in the small community of Moosejaw, Saskatchewan. His famous show, *House Party* on CBS, was one of the longest-running programs on television. Art Linkletter is also a very astute businessman with direct involvement in dozens of successful enterprises. Here are Art's most important insights for creating wealth and success.

1. I'm going to do the work I enjoy. You only live once, so do what you love.
2. There will always be difficulties, failures and challenges along the way.
3. The margin between mediocrity and success is very small and when related to time and effort, over and above what is expected.
4. I will use pull whenever I can to open the doors to opportunity, but I will make sure to work when the door is opened for me.
5. I will recognize and be alert to my own weaknesses, and find people who excel in the things where I falter.
6. I will consider an opportunity to advance more important than the immediate money and fringe benefits of the situation.
7. I will always stretch my abilities and goals a little further

than my comfort zone, within reason.
8. I will learn from my failures and then put them behind me.
9. I will follow the Golden Rule. I will not do a deal where someone else is short-changed, cheated or taken advantage of.
10. I will use other people's money provided I feel certain the money itself can grow at a faster rate than the interest charges. I will not be greedy.

"The business got into me!"

For two years he was just average — then it got into him — now he's at the top

When you meet a successful, high-achieving individual, it's a good idea to ask, "What was it that got you into the success column? Can you recall the turning point in your career?"

In his *Great Ideas* audiocassette album, the late Earl Nightingale described one of the most interesting and impressive answers he ever received. It came from a man who had been with the same company for 20 years and had risen right to the top.

"I got into the business with my company 20 years ago," the man replied, "and for the first two years nothing much happened. I was very average and not too happy, until one day the business got into me. From that time on it's been great."

The man went on to explain that, like many others starting out, he spent the first two years waiting for his job to prove itself to him. Then one day he realized it should be the other way around. It became obvious that his job offered him whatever he wanted to make of it, as long as he would prove himself. That's when the business got into him. He threw himself completely into his work, and from then on he was no longer a man with an ordinary job. He ceased to be separate and apart from his work. He and his job became one.

And perhaps this is what you should do. You will achieve great things in your work and reap commensurate rewards to the extent that you become one with what you're doing. Remember, work is what you're doing when you'd rather be doing something else! And jobs don't have futures. Only people do!

Here's what you can do:
1. Look at your work through new eyes. See benefits you might have missed.
2. Make a list of all the positives associated with your work.
3. End each day by writing on your calendar "The best thing that happened to me today."

Memo From God

TO: You
DATE: Today
SUBJECT: Yourself
REFERENCE: Life

I am God. Today I will be handling all of your problems. Please remember that I do not need your help. If life happens to deliver a situation to you that you cannot handle, do not attempt to resolve it. Kindly put it in the SFGTD (Something For God to Do) box. It will be addressed in My time, not yours. Once the matter is placed into the box, do not hold onto it.

- If you find yourself stuck in traffic; don't despair. There are people in this world for whom driving is an unheard of privilege.
- Should you have a bad day at work; think of the man who has been out of work for years.
- Should you despair over a relationship gone bad; think of the person who has never known what it's like to love and be loved in return.
- Should you grieve the passing of another weekend; think of the woman in dire straits, working twelve hours a day, seven days a week to feed her children.
- Should your car break down, leaving you miles away from assistance; think of the paraplegic who would love

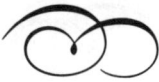

the opportunity to take that walk.
- Should you notice a new grey hair in the mirror; think of the cancer patient in chemo who wishes she had hair to examine.
- Should you find yourself at a loss and pondering what is life all about, asking what is my purpose? Be thankful. There are those who didn't live long enough to get the opportunity.
- Should you find yourself the victim of other people's bitterness, ignorance, smallness or insecurities; remember, things could be worse. You could be them!

The Millionaire

In the 1950s there was a popular television program called *The Millionaire* that featured a rich man who gave a million dollars anonymously each week to some unsuspecting person. Then we saw how the money changed the life of that individual. The outcome was often bad. Rather than solving problems or making life easier, the unexpected wealth just brought greed, violence and conflict.

Well, that was just fiction — or was it? The truth is that sudden wealth often has precisely that effect on those who achieve it. With the spread of state lotteries throughout the United States, numerous people become millionaires each year. We're seeing now what happens to those "lucky" people who hold the winning tickets.

Would you believe that one-third of all lottery winners go from rags to riches to bankruptcy? And another 25 percent wind up selling the remaining payments of their winnings at a discounted rate to pay off debts. A company called Woodbridge Sterling Capital, which buys those future payments, already holds $500 million in face-value jackpots. Richard Salvato, the CEO of that company, said, "The trouble with getting all that money is that it amplifies the person's weaknesses. If they were reckless with their ordinary paycheques, they're also reckless with the bigger ones. People just don't change."

So if you're fantasizing about winning the lottery and

living on easy street for the rest of your life, it's probably a pipe dream. First, your chances of hitting the jackpot are infinitesimal, and second — even if you do — your troubles are just beginning. I learned that from *The Millionaire* in 1955.

There are few exceptions to real success than that of hard work.

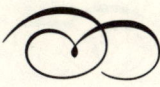

Slowdance

Have you ever watched kids
On a merry-go-round
Or listened to the rain
Lapping on the ground?
Ever followed a butterfly's erratic flight
Or gazed at the sun into the fading night?
You better slow down
Don't dance so fast
Time is short
The music won't last.
Do you run through each day on the fly?
When you ask, "How are you?"
Do you hear the reply?
When the day is done,
Do you lie in your bed
With the next hundred chores
Running through your head?
You'd better slow down
Don't dance so fast
Time is short
The music won't last.
Ever told your child,
We'll do it tomorrow
And in your haste, not see his sorrow?
Ever lost touch,

Let a good friendship die
Cause you never had time
To call and say "Hi"?
You'd better slow down
Don't dance so fast
Time is short
The music won't last.
When you run so fast to get somewhere
You miss half the fun of getting there.
When you worry and hurry through your day,
It is like an unopened gift . . .
Thrown away . . .
Life is not a race.
Do take it slower
Hear the music
Before the song is over.
— *Written by a teenage girl with cancer*

Decisions

Here's a story about the biggest decision of all — the decision to live. It's about a remarkable man, Viktor Frankl, who found himself incarcerated in a Nazi concentration camp during World War II. A prominent psychologist before the war dramatically changed his life, Frankl suffered the fate of millions of Jews — hard labour under the most awful conditions imaginable. Every day many of his fellow prisoners would die from malnutrition, savage beatings or from being herded off to the gas chambers, the ultimate humiliation.

Despite the severity of his conditions, Viktor Frankl realized there was one element that his captors could not control — his attitude. Simply stated, he chose to live. And nothing, absolutely nothing, would shift his resolve to win this greatest of human battles.

To alleviate his terrifying circumstances, he focused on a positive picture of the future. He visualized being a successful psychologist, attending concerts and enjoying a fulfilling lifestyle. Never did he allow himself to surrender to the depravation that was going on all around him. This incredible fortitude, decisiveness, persistence and strength of character eventually paid off when the war ended. Those who had nothing to live for, and there were many, did not survive. Viktor Frankl went on to become one of the world's most renowned therapists and inspirational leaders. The

book detailing his struggles, *Man's Search for Meaning*, is a classic. Make sure you read it more than once. It will uplift your soul.

— *Excerpt from* The Power of Focus
Jack Canfield, Mark Victor Hansen, Les Hewitt

Dad's Helper

A little boy was helping his father move some books out of an attic into more spacious quarters downstairs. It was important to this little boy that he was helping his dad, even though he was probably getting in the way and slowing things down more than he was actually assisting. But that boy had a wise and patient father who knew it was more important to work at a task with his young son than it was to move a pile of books efficiently.

Among this man's books, however, were some rather large study books, and it was a chore for the boy to get them down the stairs. As a matter of fact, on one particular load, the boy dropped his pile of books several times. Finally, he sat down on the stairs and wept in frustration. He wasn't strong enough to carry the big books down a narrow stairway. It hurt him to think he couldn't do this for his daddy.

Without a word, the father picked up the dropped books, put them into the boy's arms, and scooped up both the boy and the books into his arms and carried them down the stairs. And so they continued for load after load, both enjoying each other's company very much. The boy carrying the books, the dad carrying the boy.

— *Ron Mehl*

Our Deepest Fear

Our deepest fear is not that we are inadequate.
Our deepest fear is that we are powerful beyond measure.
It is our light, not our darkness that frightens us.
We ask ourselves, who am I to be brilliant, gorgeous,
    talented and fabulous?
Actually, who are we not to be?
You are a child of God.
Your playing small doesn't serve the world.
There's nothing enlightened about shrinking so that
    other people won't feel insecure around you.
We were born to make manifest the glory of God that is
    within us.
It's not just in some of us; it's in everyone.
And as we let our own light shine, we unconsciously
    give other people permission to do the same.
As we are liberated from our own fears, our presence
    automatically liberates others.

Source: A Return to Love *by Marianne Williamson*
(As quoted by Nelson Mandela in his inaugural speech, 1994)

Life's Little Instructions

Sing in the shower
Treat everyone you meet like you want to be treated
Watch a sunrise at least once a year
Leave the toilet seat in the down position
Never refuse homemade brownies
Strive for excellence, not perfection
Plant a tree on your birthday
Learn three clean jokes
Return borrowed vehicles with the gas tank full
Compliment three people every day
Never waste an opportunity to tell someone you love them
Leave everything a little better than you found it
Keep it simple
Think big thoughts but relish small pleasures
Become the most positive and enthusiastic person you know
Floss your teeth
Ask for a raise when you feel you've earned it
Be forgiving of yourself and others
Overtip breakfast waitresses
Say "Thank you" a lot
Say "Please" a lot
Avoid negative people
Buy whatever kids are selling on card tables in their front yards
Wear polished shoes

Remember other people's birthdays
Commit yourself to constant improvement
Carry jumper cables in your trunk
Have a firm handshake
Send lots of Valentine cards
Sign them "Someone who thinks you are terrific"
Look people in the eye
Be the first to say, "Hello"
Use the good silver
Return all things you borrow
Make new friends but cherish the old ones
Keep secrets
Sing in a choir
Plant flowers every spring
Have a dog
Always accept an outstretched hand
Stop blaming others
Take responsibility for every area of your life
Wave at kids on school buses
Be there when people need you
Feed a stranger's expired parking meter
Don't expect life to be fair
Never underestimate the power of love
Drink champagne for no reason at all
Live your life as an exclamation, not an explanation

Don't be afraid to say, "I made a mistake"
Don't be afraid to say, "I don't know"
Compliment even small improvements
Keep your promises (no matter what)
Marry only for love
Rekindle old friendships
Count your blessings
Call your mother

On Being Poor

One day a father of a very wealthy family took his son on a trip to the country with the firm purpose of showing his son how poor people can be. They spent a couple of days and nights on the farm of what would be considered a very poor family.

On their return from their trip, the father asked his son, "How was the trip?"

"It was great, Dad."

"Did you see how poor people can be?" the father asked.

"Oh yeah," said the son.

"So what did you learn from the trip?" asked the father.

The son answered, "I saw that we have one dog and they had four. We have a pool that reaches to the middle of our garden and they have a creek that has no end. We have imported lanterns in our garden and they have the stars at night. Our patio reaches to the front yard and they have the whole horizon. We have a small piece of land to live on and they have fields that go beyond our sight. We have servants who serve us, but they serve others. We buy our food, but they grow theirs. We have walls around our property to protect us, they have friends to protect them."

With this the boy's father was speechless.

Then his son added, "Thanks Dad, for showing me how poor we are."

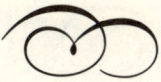

Too many times we forget what we have and concentrate on what we don't have. What is one person's worthless object is another's prize possession. It is all based on one's perspective. Makes you wonder what would happen if we all gave thanks to God for all the bounty we have been provided, instead of worrying about wanting more.

— *Unknown*

Quiz

1. Name the five wealthiest people in the world.
2. Name the last five Heisman trophy winners.
3. Name the last five winners of the Miss America contest.
4. Name ten people who have won the Nobel or Pulitzer Prize.
5. Name the last half dozen Academy Award winners for best actor and actress.
6. Name the last decade's worth of World Series winners.

How did you do?

The point is, none of us remember the headliners of yesterday. These are no second-rate achievers. They are the best in their fields. But the applause dies. Awards tarnish. Achievements are forgotten. Accolades and certificates are buried with their owners.

Here's another quiz. See how you do on this one.

1. List a few teachers who aided your journey through school.
2. Name three friends who have helped you through a difficult time.
3. Name five people who have taught you something worthwhile.

4. Think of a few people who have made you feel appreciated and special.
5. Think of five people you enjoy spending time with.
6. Name half a dozen heroes whose stories have inspired you.

Easier? You bet.

The people who make a difference in your life are not the ones with the most credentials, the most money or the most awards. They are the ones who care.

The Importance of the Subconscious Mind

In his book *The Wisdom of Your Subconscious Mind,* John K. Williams says there are four powers of the subconscious mind that we must all remember:

1. You are the architect of your destiny. Every experience in your life — health, illness, poverty, wealth, failure and success — is the result of actions or purposes you set in motion.
2. You have creative power in your life because you can visualize what you want to achieve so clearly that it becomes imprinted on the subconscious mind — which then brings the dream to reality.
3. You are a radiating power able to attract to yourself everything you want, providing that you are willing to pay the price.
4. You are the building and directing power of your life. There's nothing that is — that has been — which isn't dependent on the power of the mind. When life presents you with a challenge, it is up to you to meet that challenge. Whether you fail or succeed is up to you and you alone.

Some people pay the price of success, but don't pay the price to stay there.

Grow Yourself...

11 Powerful Ways To Expand Your Life

1. Define your future. Describe the life you'd like to live. The future you see defines the person you'll need to be. Identify the traits and qualities you'd like to acquire. Think bigger than yourself. An acorn that only thinks as an acorn will never become a mighty oak. Stretch yourself. You are undoubtedly capable of more than you ever dreamed is possible for you.

2. Become the person who would achieve your goals. As you develop the skills, knowledge, relationships and demeanour of the "future you," your goals will be the natural byproduct of your growth. Spend an extra hour each day in the study of your chosen field.

3. Give more than you must. Nothing advances until somebody does more than they are paid to do. Always deliver more value than the others expect. Don't require others to acknowledge your generosity. Give with "class."

4. Make time for what you love. If you don't live fully, you deny the world your potential contributions. Your "play" sometimes contributes as much as your "work." What you love reveals the value you bring to the world.

5. Refine your Inner Circle. We define ourselves through our key relationships. Explore the mix and depth of those with whom you spend most of your time. Release those who limit you and connect with those who can

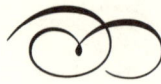

help you live more fully.
6. Resolve your unfinished business. Either deal with it or discard it. Say your apologies, face your fears, pay your debts, express your gratitude and get on with living. Don't let yesterday drain value from today and tomorrow. Break out of the limited world of your past and start to grow.
7. Rethink existing habits and routines. Describe your typical day and then reconsider every aspect of it. Change or expand the places you go, people you see, things you do and the time you devote to each. Try new things. Learn a new language, go someplace different, do some things you'd typically pass by. Find out what your possibilities really are.
8. Lighten up. Stop stressing over things that only matter to you emotionally. When life isn't fair to you, get over it quickly. Take your misfortunes as "course corrections" rather than "catastrophes." Let go so you can grow.
9. Tighten up. Sloppiness in life allows more variables to creep in and spoil your plans. Stay on target, increase your self-discipline, and master the art of self-motivation. Sometimes details matter a lot.
10. Profile yourself. Keep a journal of your goals, concerns, fears and dreams. Review it at least once a year. Look for patterns that reveal your core values, natural velocity,

    natural intelligences and recurring situations. Realize how life ebbs and flows for you. Notice the natural cycles of life. Know yourself.

11. Invest in yourself. Set aside a portion of each year's income to acquire new tools and teachers to increase your potential. Refine your systems, get expert coaching, attend special conferences, cultivate a study group, appoint a board of advisors. You are your only true asset. Send part of today ahead to the person you'll be in the future.

— The Acorn Principle
Jim Cathcart

The Golden Ladder of Giving

To give reluctantly.

To give cheerfully, but not
in proportion to the need.

To give cheerfully, and proportionately,
but not until solicited.

To give cheerfully, proportionately,
and unsolicited, but to put the gift into
the poor person's hand, thus creating
shame.

To give in such a way that the
distressed may know their benefactors,
without being known to them.

To know the objects of our bounty,
but remain unknown to them.

To give so that the benefactor may not
know those who have been relieved,
and they shall not know him.

To prevent poverty by teaching a
trade, setting a person up in business,
or in some other way preventing the
need of charity. This is the highest step
in charity's golden ladder.

— *Maimonides*
(12th Century Jewish Scholar)

Be happy, optimistic and live a longer, healthier life

Optimists, on average, live longer than pessimists, and optimism can lead to success at work, school, sports, and better health, a Mayo clinic study suggests.

"What is happening in the mind is strongly influencing the body, or the final outcome of the body, which is death," said Toshihiko Maruta, a Mayo psychiatrist and one of the authors of the study in the journal *Mayo Clinic Proceedings*.

The research is derived from questionnaires answered by clinic patients and more than 800 Olmstead county residents between 1962 and 1965. Follow-up questionnaires show that regardless of age or sex, the most pessimistic among them tended to die earlier than the most optimistic.

Maruta's research didn't surprise David Lykken, professor of psychology at the University of Minnesota and author of the book *Happiness*.

"It's a well-known fact that happy people don't get sick as often, and, when they do get sick or injured, they recover more quickly," he said. "That is thought to be one of the main reasons why we tend to be a happy breed. Grouches and grumblers didn't do as well when they got sick or were searching for a mate. Nobody wants to be around them."

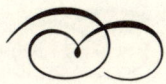

How To Spend Your Dash

I read of a man who stood to speak
At the funeral of a friend.
He referred to the dates on her tombstone
From the beginning . . . to the end.

He noted that first came her date of birth
And spoke the following date with tears,
But he said what mattered most of all
Was the dash between those years. (1900-1970)

For that dash represents all the time
That she spent alive on earth . . .
And now only those who loved her
Know what that little line is worth.

For it matters not, how much we own;
The cars, the house, the cash,
What matters is how we live and love
And how we spend our dash.

So think about this long and hard . . .
Are there things you'd like to change?
For you never know how much time is left,
That can still be rearranged.

If we could just slow down enough
To consider what's true and real,
And always try to understand
The way other people feel.

And be less quick to anger,
And show appreciation more
And love the people in our lives
Like we've never loved before.

If we treat each other with respect,
And more often wear a smile . . .
Remembering that this special dash
Might only last a little while.

So, when your eulogy's being read
With your life's actions to rehash . . .
Would you be proud of the things they say
About how you spent your dash?
— *Author Unknown*

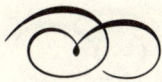

Thinking Does Make It So!

The theme of choosing our thoughts and choosing our future is a timeless leadership principle that echoes throughout the ages. Marcus Aurelius, the second-century philosopher and Roman emperor who wrote the classic *Meditations,* said simply, "Our life is what our thoughts make it." In the 16th century, William Shakespeare observed that "there's nothing good or bad but thinking makes it so." In his 19th century *Journals,* Ralph Waldo Emerson wrote, "Life consists of what a man is thinking of all day." In 1871, Charles Darwin wrote, "the highest possible stage in moral culture is when we recognize that we ought to control our thoughts."

Core truths are regularly rediscovered and restated for their time. At the dawn of the 20th century, William James, the American philosopher and "father of modern psychology," declared, "The greatest discovery of my generation is that human beings can alter their lives by altering their attitudes of mind."

In computer programming, "source code" consists of human-readable statements, which are translated into a machine code that computers can read. Computers then execute or act upon these instructions. Our own thoughts — the beginning point of all our choices — is like our personal source code that we execute or translate into action. Our thoughts set our programming instructions.

If we continue to think like we've always thought, we'll continue to get what we've always got.
1. Our daily thought choices translate into our daily actions.
2. Our actions accumulate to form our habits.
3. Our habits form our character.
4. Our character attracts our circumstances.
5. Our circumstances determine our future.

Taking responsibility for our choices starts with choosing our thoughts.

Part II

We don't need to understand
first to believe.
We must believe first in order
to understand.
— *St. Augustine*

The rocks and boulders in the stream
give it its song.
— *Unknown*

The true meaning of life is to plant trees,
under whose shade you do not expect to sit.
— *Nelson Henderson*

You can't build a reputation on
what you are going to do.
— *Henry Ford*

A man can stand almost anything
other than a succession of ordinary days.
— *Johann Wolfgang von Goethe*

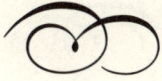

The greater the dream,
the greater the potential.
— *E. Paul Houby*

Everyone gets an idea in the shower.
But the successful ones get out of the shower,
dry off and do something about it.
— *Nolan Bushnell*
Founder of Atari

The great thing about this world is not so much
where we are but in what direction we are moving .
— *Oliver Wendell Holmes*

Vision is the world's most desperate need.
There are no hopeless situations
only people who think hopelessly.
— *Winifred Newman*

Don't regret growing old for it is a privilege denied to many.
— *Irish Proverb*

Be not afraid of going slowly;
Be only afraid of standing still.
— *Chinese Proverb*

My great concern is not whether you have failed,
but whether you are content with your failure.
— *Abraham Lincoln*

It's what you learn after you know it all that counts.
— *John Wooden*
UCLA Basketball Coach

It is not enough to say no to things that frighten us.
We must find worthwhile causes
to which we care to say yes.
— *Joseph Campbell*
Philosopher

Everything that is really great and inspiring
is created by the individual who can labor in freedom.
— *Albert Einstein*

It's been my observation that most successful people
get ahead during the time other people waste.
— *Henry Ford*

If a person will spend one hour a day
on the same subject for five years,
that person will be an expert on that subject.
— *Earl Nightingale*

Don't let your learning lead to knowledge.
Let your learning lead to action.
— *Jim Rohn*

It is never too late to be what you might have become.
— *George Eliot*

Do not let what you cannot do
interfere with what you can do.
— *John Wooden*

Winning is a habit, unfortunately so is losing.
— *Vince Lombardi, Coach, NFL Green Bay Packers*

The secret of getting ahead is getting started.
The secret of getting started is breaking your complex
overwhelming tasks
into small manageable tasks, and then starting
on the first one.
— *Mark Twain*

Success will not wait.
If I delay she will become betrothed to another
And lost to me forever.
This is the time.
This is the place.
I will act now.
— *Og Mandino*

If you don't get what you want, it is either a sign
either that you did not seriously want it,
or that you tried to bargain over the price.
— *Rudyard Kipling*

Success is not measured by what a man accomplishes
but by the opposition he has encountered and
the courage with which he has maintained
the struggle against overwhelming odds.
— *Charles Lindbergh, Aviator*

I know God will not give me anything I can't handle.
I just wish he didn't trust me so much.
— *Mother Teresa*

There are no shortcuts to any place worth going.
— *Beverly Sills, Opera Singer*

There is no substitute for character.
You can buy brains, but you can't buy character.
— *Robert A. Cook*

Do something every day that you don't want to do.
This is the golden rule for acquiring the habit
of doing your duty without pain.
— *Mark Twain*

The reason so many people never get anywhere in life
is because when opportunity knocks,
they are out in the backyard looking for four-leaf clovers.
— *Walter P. Chrysler*

Failure is the opportunity to begin again more intelligently.
— *Henry Ford*

Do what you can, with what you have where you are.
— *President Theodore Roosevelt*

No matter what a person's past may have been,
his future is spotless.
— *Unknown*

If what you did yesterday still looks pretty big to you,
then you haven't done enough today.
— *Earl Wilson*

You never work for somebody else.
Someone else might sign your check,
but you're the one who fills in the amount.
— *Zig Ziglar*

Being cheerful keeps you healthy.
— *King Solomon*

Remember, happiness doesn't depend upon
who you are or what you have;
it depends solely upon what you think.
— *Dave Campbell*

When a happy person comes into the room,
it is as if another candle has been lit.
— *Ralph Waldo Emerson*

Any fact facing us is not as important
as our attitude toward it,
for that determines our success or failure.
— *Norman Vincent Peale*

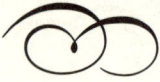

No one is useless in this world
who lightens the burden of it to anyone else.
— *Charles Dickens*

Art is to beauty what honour is to honesty.
— *Sir Winston Churchill*

There is a loftier ambition than
merely to stand high in the world;
it is to stoop down and lift mankind a little higher.
— *Henry Van Dyke*

You cannot escape the responsibility of tomorrow
by evading it today.
— *Abraham Lincoln*

You will always move in the direction
of your currently dominant thoughts.
— *Dr. Denis Waitley*

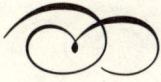

This above all: to thine own self be true,
and it must follow, as the night the day,
thou canst not then be false to any man.
— *Hamlet, William Shakespeare*

Before anything else, getting ready is the secret of success.
— *Henry Ford*

The family is the first essential cell of human society.
— *Pope John XXIII*

Often a recession is all in your mind.
— *Unknown*

The battle of Waterloo was won on the playing fields of Eton.
— *Arthur Wellesley, Duke of Wellington*

If you don't drive your business
you will be driven out of business.
— *B.C. Forbes*

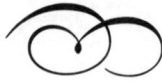

If you can establish yourself as an expert,
buyers will come to you,
instead of the other way around.
— *Unknown*

I keep six honest-serving men
(they taught me all I knew)
Their names are what and why and when
and how and where and who.
— *Rudyard Kipling*

Lots of people want to ride with you in your limo,
But what you want is someone who will
take the bus with you when your limo breaks down.
— *Oprah Winfrey*

We should get into the habit of reading inspirational books,
looking at inspirational pictures,
hearing inspirational music,
associating with inspirational friends.
— *Alfred A. Montapert*

Live as if you were to die tomorrow.
Learn as if you were to live forever.
— *Mahatma Gandhi*

We're about as happy as we make up our minds to be.
— *Abraham Lincoln*

Good actions get good results in time.
— *Dr. Denis Waitley*

Negative thinking always repels;
it consistently produces negative consequences.
— *Paul J. Meyer*

All of life is action and passion
and not to be involved in the actions
and passions of your time
is to risk having not really lived at all.
— *Herodotus, Greek Historian*

Make no useless acquaintances.
— *Baron Rothschild*

Only the true competent person
can rise above politics.
— *Peter Drucker*

Do you value life? Then waste not time,
for that is the stuff of which life is made.
— *Benjamin Franklin*

What you dwell upon grows...
...so be careful.
— *Brian Tracy*

Act as if it were impossible to fail and it shall be.
— *Dorothy Brandle*

In order to achieve things you've never achieved before
you must be willing to do things you've never done before.
— *Unknown*

It is continually viewing yourself as a
do-it-to-yourself project.
— *Dr. Denis Waitley*

Our great business is not to see
what lies daily at a distance
but to do what lies clearly at hand.
— *Thomas Carlyle*

Whatever you vividly imagine,
ardently desire,
sincerely believe,
and enthusiastically act upon
must inevitably come to pass.
— *Paul J. Meyer*

If honesty did not exist it would have been invented
as it is the surest way of getting rich.
— *Earl Nightingale*

The more that is given,
the less people will work for themselves.
— *Leo Tolstoy*

Success is 2% inspiration and 98% perspiration.
— *Thomas Edison*

Remember — you can't accomplish it on the outside
until you become it on the inside.
— *Brian Tracy*

The first qualification for success in my view
is a strong work ethic.
— *Henry Ford II*

Work is life and good work is good life.
— *James W. Elliott*

There is one thing stronger than all the armies in the world,
And that is an idea whose time has come.
— *Victor Hugo*

No man is an island entire of itself.
— *John Donne, English poet*

Carpe diem! (Seize the day)

You can't tell what you don't know
any more than you can come back
from where you've never been.
— *Unknown*

Wise men store up knowledge.
— *King Solomon, Proverbs 10:14*

Creativity is looking at what everyone else looks at
but seeing what no one else sees.
— *Paul J. Meyer*

The constant force of the wind twists a giant tree
into a shape entirely different from its nature.
— *Unknown*

When you have to make a choice and don't make it,
that in itself is a choice.
— *William James*

The same hammer that shatters the glass forges the steel.
— *Russian Proverb*

You will find yourself by losing yourself in service
to other people, your country and your God.
— *Mahatma Gandhi*

Difficulties mastered are opportunities won.
— *Sir Wiinston Churchill*

Your imagination is your preview of
life's coming attractions.
— *Dr. Denis Waitley*

You cannot consistently perform in a manner
that is inconsistent with the way you see yourself.
— *Dr. Joyce Brothers*

If you have an ability that goes beyond providing
for your own needs,
you have a responsibility to use that ability to reach down
and help those up who do not have that capacity.
As a matter of fact, if you don't reach down
and help lift up those less fortunate,
the day will come when due to sheer weight of numbers,
they will reach up and pull you down.
— *Coach Jobie Harris,*
Zig Ziglars Junior College, History Teacher

You can have everything in life you want
if you will just help enough other people
get what they want.
— *credited to Zig Ziglar and Charles Swindoll*

Golf Is Life
I found out that all the important lessons of life
are contained in the three rules
for achieving a perfect golf swing.
1. Keep your head down.
2. Follow through.
3. Be born with money.
— *P.J. O'Rourke*

The measure of success is not whether you have a tough
problem to deal with,
But whether it's the same problem you had last year.
— *John Foster*

The deepest craving of any human being
is to be appreciated.
— *William James*

No one can make you feel bad without your consent.
— *Eleanor Roosevelt*

I never met a man I didn't like.
— *Will Rogers*

The last of human freedoms is to choose one's attitude
in any given set of circumstances.
— *Viktor Frankl*

Not all readers become leaders. But all leaders must be readers.
— *Harry S. Truman*

The books you don't read won't help.
— *Jim Rohn*

Take a coin from your purse and invest it in your mind.
It will come pouring out of your mind and
overflow your purse.
— *Benjamin Franklin*

Criticism is easy; achievement is difficult.
— *Sir Winston Churchill*

Whenever two people meet there are really six people present.
There is each man as he sees himself,
each man as the other sees him,
and each man as he really is.
— *William James*

To be conscious of what we are perceiving or thinking
is to be conscious of our own existence.
— *Aristotle*

It is even harder for the average ape to believe
he has descended from man.
— *H.L. Merke*

After the ship has sunk, everyone knows
how she might have been saved.
— *Italian Proverb*

The key to success is always remembering
where you came from
and how much you dread going back there.
— *Twyman Towery, PhD*

Beware of stalls lest the ground come up and smite thee.
— *Old Airline Bush Pilot*

The block of granite which is an obstacle on
the path of the weak
becomes a stepping stone on the path of the strong.
— *Thomas Carlyle*

The Talmud says that at first a bad habit enters our lives
as an invited guest but before long
becomes a member of the family
and ultimately ends up taking over the house,
and we come to feel that we have lost a precious part
of who we are and who we want to be.

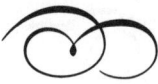

Few of us can do great things
but all of us can do small things with great love.
— *Mother Teresa*

Whether I shall turn out to be the hero of my own life
or whether that station will be held by anybody else,
these pages must show.
— *Opening line of* David Copperfield
Charles Dickens

Never lie,
defend what you believe in
and admit your mistakes quickly
— *Phil Klein*
Father to Alberta Premier Ralph Klein
The only three bits of advice passed to his eldest son

The first responsibility of a leader is to define reality.
— *Max De Pree*

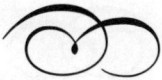

If you want to make a big difference be confident.
If you want to make a big difference be credible.
If you want to make a big difference speak to people's needs.
If you want to make a big difference don't be afraid
To do something even if it seems small.
— *John C. Maxwell, Author*
Running with the Giants

Success is not final.
Failure is not fatal:
It is the courage to continue that counts.
— *Sir Winston Churchill*

Those of you who will be truly happy are the ones
who have sought and found a way to serve.
— *Albert Schweitzer*

All our knowledge has its origin in our perception.
— *Leonardo da Vinci*

Only the dead have seen the end of war.
— *Plato*

He who reigns within himself and rules his passions, desires and fears is more than a King.
— *Milton*

The secret of success in life is for a man to be ready for his opportunity when it comes.
— *Benjamin Disraeli*
19th-century Prime Minister of Great Britain

Imagination rules the world.
— *Napoleon Bonaparte*

Integrity without knowledge is weak and useless.
— *Samuel Johnson*

An officer who is afraid of failure will never win!
Any man who is afraid to die will never really live.
— *General George Patton*

Too many failures are traced to a lack of persistence
and not lack of talent or ability.
— *Dr. Paul Parker*

We have a long time to sleep when we're dead.
— *Benjamin Franklin*

Men do not fail:
they give up trying.
— *Elihu Root*

Much like marriage — commitment to one endeavour
is critical for long-term success.
— *Anonymous*

Leadership is the ability to decide what has to be done
and then get people who want to do it.
— *General Dwight D. Eisenhower*

When you lose a customer, you lose in two ways:
First, you don't get their money.
Second, your competitor does.
— *Bill Gates*

I will spend an hour editing an eight-word sentence into five.
— *Jerry Seinfeld*

The only thing I ever wanted in business
is an unfair advantage.
— *Patricia Fripp, CPAE*
Professional Speaker — Author

A lot of people die at forty but are not buried
until thirty years later.
— *General George Patton*

You can't be lucky for 30 years.
Longevity and commitment to a single purpose
will win the day.
— *Peter Legge*

We overestimate what we can do in one year —
But we underestimate what we can do in five years.
— *Peter Drucker*

When God wants to send you a gift he sends you a problem.
— *Norman Vincent Peale*

1,000 excuses for failure.
Never a good reason.
— *Mark Twain*

When was the last time you did something
for the first time?
— *Linda Edgecombe*
Author and Professional Speaker

The first sign of success is thankfulness.
— *Charlie "T" Jones*

To achieve something you have never achieved before
you must become someone you have never been before.
— *Les Brown*

Opportunities?
I make opportunities.
— *Napoleon Bonaparte*

I believe that leadership is the ability to solve problems.
— *General Colin Powell*

What is past is prologue.
— *William Shakespeare*

You can tell a big person by the way he treats little people.
— *Thomas Carlyle*

A wise man will make more opportunities than he finds.
— *Francis Bacon*

Patience and foresight are the two most important qualities in business.
— *Henry Ford*

Success in war depends upon the golden rule of war. Speed — simplicity — boldness.
— *General George S. Patton*

What gets rewarded gets done.
— *Michael LeBoeuf*

Leaders think about the future.
— *Peter Drucker*

When I was young I observed that nine out of every ten things I did were failures so I did ten times more work.
— *George Bernard Shaw*

Next to excellence is the appreciation of it.
— *William Makepeace Thackeray*

What is Leadership

To guide.
To direct.
To begin.
To be chief.
To influence.
To command.
To be the first.
To go ahead of.
To create a path.
To show the way.
To control actions.
To cause progress.
— *Danny Cox*
Professional Speaker and Author
Leadership When the Heat's On

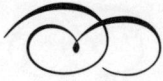

The Pareto Principle:
20% of your priorities will give you 80% of your production
IF
you spend your time, energy, money and
personnel on the top 20% of your priorities.

That which holds our attention determines our action.
— *William James*

We judge ourselves by what we feel capable of doing:
while others judge us by what we have already done.
— *Henry Wadsworth Longfellow*

In the matters of principle, stand like a rock;
In matters of taste, swim with the current.
— *Thomas Jefferson*

When your time is worth dollars, don't do penny jobs.
— *Mary Kay Ash*

Man's greatness lies in the power of thought.
— *Blaise Pascal*
(1623-1662)

The first requisite of success is the ability
to apply your physical
and mental energies to one problem without growing weary.
— *Thomas Edison*

To have more — you must first be more.
— *Johann Wolfgang von Goethe*

The potential of the average person is like
a huge ocean unsailed,
a new continent unexplored,
a world of possibilities waiting to be released
and channelled toward some great good.
— *Brian Tracy*

The deepest principle of human nature
is the craving to be appreciated
and the desire to be important.
— *William James*

If we're content being average consider this:

Best
|
Average
|
Worst

We are the worst of the best or the best of the worst.
Decide right now to be the best you can
and do whatever it takes to be the best.
— *Unknown*

Planning for tomorrow means sloughing off yesterday.
Before you can do something new
you have to stop doing something old.
— *Peter Drucker*

Circumstances do not make the man;
they merely reveal him to himself.
— *Epictetus*

No success in public life can compensate
for failure in the home.
— *Benjamin Disraeli*

Work on yourself as if your future depended upon it,
because it does.
— *Brian Tracy*

Praise Is Powerful:
I have discovered a remarkable thing;
men will die for a ribbon
— *Napoleon Bonaparte*

It takes only 13 muscles to smile and 112 to frown.
— *Unknown*

A man without a smile should not open a shop.
— *Chinese Proverb*

Decide exactly what you want to do in life
and then act as if it were impossible to fail.
— *Unknown*

Confidence is the directness and courage
in meeting the facts of life.
— *John Dewey*

More powerful than the will to win
is the courage to begin.
— *Unknown*

Success seems to be largely a matter
of hanging on after others have let go.
— *William Feather*

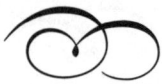

Destiny is not a matter of chance
...it is a thing to be achieved.
— *William Jennings Bryan*

He that can have patience can have what he will.
— *Benjamin Franklin*

You can't cross the sea merely by staring at the water.
— *Rabindranath Tagore*

If a man must move the world he must first move himself.
— *Socrates*

The only thing in the world worse than being talked about
...is not being talked about.
— *Unknown*

What are the three kinds of people?

1. Those who make things happen.
2. Those who watch things happen.
3. Those who wonder what happened.
— *Unknown*

Learn to work harder on your own personal growth than anything else.
— *Jim Rohn*

Fear kills more people than death.
— *General George Patton*

Every production of genius must be the production of enthusiasm.
— *Benjamin Disraeli*

Children have more need of models than of critics.
— *Joseph Joubert*

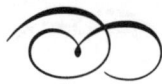

All of us, whether rich or poor, young or old,
educated or not so educated,
are the sum total of all those people and events
that have touched us since first entering this world.
Every thought we've entertained has had its effect upon
what we are now.
Every movie we've watched had its effect.
Every book or magazine we've ever read.
Every TV show has had its effect.
Every disappointment,
every triumph,
every doubt,
every dream,
every love
...each had their effect.
What we are and what we have,
we have slowly brought upon ourselves.
— *Jim Rohn*

Who decides whether you shall be happy or unhappy?
The answer — you do!
You make up your own mind how happy you will be.
— *Abraham Lincoln*

Your growth determines who you are.
Who you are determines who you attract.
Who you attract determines the success of your organization.
— *John C. Maxwell*

The best time to plant a tree is 25 years ago...
the second best time is today.
— *A Nursery in Canada*

The first and best victory is to conquer self.
— *Plato*

You can transform something important into
something urgent,
if you wait long enough.
— *Danny Cox*

Leadership is like beauty — it's hard to define
but you know it when you see it.
— *Warren Bennis*

Don't worry about the money. It will come.
Don't worry about the reputation. It will come.
Worry about the content of what you are presenting.
That is everything.
— *Dave Broadfoot*
Comedian

Worse than being blind is to see and have no vision.
— *Helen Keller*

If the vision is clear the passion comes.
— *Anonymous*

The unexamined life is not worth living.
— *Socrates*

Consider the possibilities not the limitations.
— *Anonymous*

Ideas control the world.
— *James A. Garfield*

The miserable hath no other medicine but only hope.
— *William Shakespeare*

In all things it is better to hope than to despair.
— *Johann Wolfgang von Goethe*

Habit is the deepest law of human nature.
— *Thomas Carlyle*

The price of greatness is responsibility.
— *Sir Winston Churchill*

Every oak was once an acorn.
— *Unknown*

Better to light a candle than curse the darkness.
— *From the "Windows of Hope" service at Westminster Abbey*

Part III

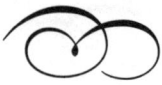

Coincidence

Abraham Lincoln was elected to Congress in 1846.
John F. Kennedy was elected to Congress in 1946.
Abraham Lincoln was elected President in 1860.
John F. Kennedy was elected President in 1960.

The names Lincoln and Kennedy each contain seven letters.
Both were particularly concerned with civil rights.
Both wives lost their children while living in the White House.
Both Presidents were shot on a Friday.
Both were shot in the head.

Lincoln's secretary was named Kennedy.
Kennedy's secretary was named Lincoln.

Both were assassinated by Southerners.
Both were succeeded by Southerners.
Both successors were named Johnson.
Andrew Johnson, who succeeded Lincoln, was born in 1808.
Lyndon Johnson, who succeeded Kennedy, was born in 1908.

John Wilkes Booth, who assassinated Lincoln,
    was born in 1839.
Lee Harvey Oswald, who assassinated Kennedy,
    was born in 1939.

Both assassins were known by their three names.
Both names are comprised of fifteen letters.

Booth ran from the theatre and was caught
    in a warehouse.
Oswald ran from a warehouse and was caught
    in a theatre.
Booth and Oswald were assassinated before their trials.

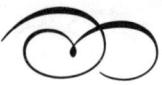

Take Time!

Take time to work — It is the price of success.
Take time to think — It is the source of power.
Take time to play — It is the secret of youth.
Take time to read — It is the foundation of wisdom.
Take time to be friendly — It's the way to happiness.
Take time to dream — Hitch your wagon to a star.
Take time to love and be loved — It is a privilege.
Take time to look around — It's too short a day to be selfish.
Take time to laugh — It is the music of your soul.

Reason to Celebrate

I had the pleasure of watching my ten-year-old nephew's final soccer game of the season. They were not doing well — they were losing 10-0 with two minutes left.

But then they got a break and scored. The team went crazy! The parents went crazy! The coaches went crazy! Everybody was jumping up and down as if they had won the championship.

When the kids came off the field, I caught up to my nephew as the celebrations continued. Puzzled, I asked, "What's going on?"

"You don't understand," he said. "That's the only goal we scored all year."

— *Sharon Major, Deer Lake, Nfld.*

Tell me, I'll forget

Show me, I may remember

Involve me and I'll understand

Anything worth doing is worth practising. If you want to enjoy doing what you love, you will want to take the time to practise it.

Practice is great for freeing yourself to explore new ways of doing things. If you are practising it means you give yourself the chance to play at something until you get it right, whatever that means to you. We learn best by getting involved in something, knowing it inside and out.

When we practise our art, we become comfortable with our talents and we put more energy into doing than into thinking about doing.

— *Submitted by L. Ahmed*

One & Only You

Every single blade of grass
And every flake of snow
Is just a wee bit different
There's no two alike you know.
From something small like grains of sand
To each gigantic star
Each were made with this in mind
To be just what they are.
How foolish then to imitate
How useless to pretend
When each of us comes from a mind
Whose ideas never end.
There'll only be just one of me
To show what I can do
And you should likewise be quite proud
There's only one of you!

To the early birds, Life's a hoot

Do you consider yourself a "morning person" or are you more of a "night owl"? In the ongoing rivalry between morning people and night owls, it looks like the a.m.'s just might have an edge.

A recent Gallup poll found this:
56% of those polled said they are morning people
and another 25% said they would like to be.
It's no wonder. Those who call themselves morning people also seem to share these traits:
They have more energy than most people
(53% vs. 39% for night owls)
They eat well (55% vs. 39%)
They lead an active lifestyle (74% vs. 64%)
They are more optimistic than most (66% vs. 56%)
They exercise more than most people (45% vs. 37%)

The Measurement of History

Of those to whom much is given, much is required.
And when at some future date the high court of history sits in judgement on each of us — recording whether in our brief span of service we fulfilled our responsibilities — our success or failure, we will be measured by the answers to four questions —
were we truly men of courage . . .
were we truly men of judgement . . .
were we truly men of integrity . . .
were we truly men of dedication?

— *John F. Kennedy*

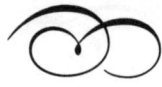

Words to the Wise

Yesterday is a cancelled cheque,

Tomorrow is a promissory note,

Today is the only cash you have —

So spend it wisely.

— *Submitted by Millie Warren, CGA*
Canada Wide Magazines & Communications Ltd.

Self Test

Check the one *best answer to each question:*

1. When you have a desire to accomplish your goal, a good combination that will help you accomplish it would be:
a) synthetic — creative imagination
b) willpower and persistence
c) love and desire
d) faith and love

2. One of the major causes of failure is the lack of:
a) persistence
b) faith
c) love
d) work

3. The starting point of all achievement is:
a) desire
b) imagination
c) positive mental attitude
d) education

How did you do? Answers on the next page.

Answers

b) willpower and persistence

a) persistence

c) positive mental attitude

Bourgeois

Too many people spend money they haven't earned, to buy things they don't want, to impress people they don't like.

Some people make slaves out of themselves by joining the bourgeoisie. What happens is that they become overly concerned with possessions, and they demand respectability for being conventional — being the same as someone else and fitting in.

Slaves work for someone else's good. Bourgeois slaves are working to impress someone else or keep up with what others are doing so that they are not free to be themselves and do what they really want.

Joining the bourgeoisie is a sidetrack to avoid living your own life. Some people don't even realize they've fallen in to the trap of convention. It takes so much time and energy to run around a treadmill, they forget that they can choose to go out and go forward.

I Would...

I would be true for there are those who trust me;

I would be pure, for there are those who care;

I would be strong, for there is much to suffer;

I would be brave, for there is much to dare;

I would be friend of all — the poor, the friendless;

I would be giving and forget the gift;

I would be humble, for I know my weakness;

I would look up — and laugh, and love, and lift.

— *Author Unknown*

The 10 Rules for Being Human

1. You will receive a body.
2. You will be presented with lessons.
3. There are almost no mistakes, only lessons.
4. Lessons are repeated until learned.
5. Learning does not end.
6. There is no better place than here.
7. Others are only mirrors of you.
8. What you make of your life is up to you.
9. All the answers lie inside of you.
10. You will forget all of these rules at your birth.

From If Life Is A Game Then These Are The Rules
By Cherie Carter-Scott, Ph.D.

11 Commandments for an Enthusiastic Team

1. Help each other be right — not wrong.
2. Look for ways to make new ideas work — not for reasons they won't.
3. If in doubt — check it out. Don't make negative assumptions about each other.
4. Help each other win and take pride in each other's victories.
5. Speak positively about each other and about your organization at every opportunity.
6. Maintain a positive mental attitude no matter what the circumstances.
7. Act with initiative and courage as it all depends on you.
8. Do everything with enthusiasm — it's contagious.
9. Share the glory; to get credit — give it away.
10. Don't lose faith — never give up.
11. Love what you do — have fun!

These are the 11 Commandments of Envision Credit Union

Leadership

The challenge of leadership is to be strong,
Not rude,
Be kind, but not weak
Be bold, but not a bully
Be thoughtful, but not lazy
Be humble, but not timid
Be proud, but not arrogant
Have humour but without folly
Then I know that the only way
things are going to change for me
Is when I change.

Cleaning House

Housework is an inner as well as an outer activity.

Many of us spend a good deal of time ordering and straightening our physical environments while forgetting to do the same for our mental/emotional living spaces.

We need to go regularly into the closets and storage spaces of our lives to clear out the old and make room for the new. Do we have old debts that need to be taken care of? People whom we need to comfort, reconnect with, or let go of? Projects that either need to be completed or released? Beliefs that are no longer relevant to our current situation?

The more clutter we accumulate in our lives, the more overwhelmed we feel and the more difficult it becomes to sort things out. But when we take the time to clean house and free ourselves from old burdens, we can experience the lightness of being that allows us to move, effortlessly and joyously on to new goals and experiences.

A Hug

If I could catch a rainbow
I would do it just for you
And share with you its beauty
On the days you're feeling blue
If I could build a mountain
You could call your very own
A place to find serenity
A place to be alone
If I could take your troubles
I would toss them in the sea
But all these things I'm finding
Are impossible for me
I cannot build a mountain
Or catch a rainbow fair
But let me be what I know best
A friend that's always there.

Laughter Makes the World Go Round

The value of a smile is priceless. It transcends race, occupation, age and gender to connect all living beings.

She knew what all smart women knew:
Laughter made you live better and longer.
— *Gail Parent*

The most wasted of all days is one without laughter.
— *E.E. Cummings*

He who laughs, lasts.
— *Mary Pettibone Poole*

I think laughter may be a form of courage. As humans we sometimes stand tall and look into the sun and laugh, and I think we are never more brave than when we do that.
— *Linda Ellerbee*

He has achieved success who has lived well, laughed often, and loved much.
— *Bessie Anderson Stanley*

A good laugh is sunshine in a house.
— *William Makepeace Thackeray*

The human race has one really effective weapon and that is laughter.
— *Mark Twain*

Time spent laughing is time spent with the Gods.
— *Japanese Proverbs*

A good laugh is as good as a prayer.
— *L.M. Montgomery*

If you could choose one characteristic that would get you through life, choose a sense of humour.
— *Jennifer Jones*

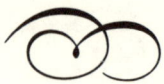

Success is Yours

Start with A...
Avoid working for power and money.
Be honest, reliable, faithful and aggressive.
Choose your friends carefully.
Don't be afraid to take risks.
Establish goals and work systematically toward achieving them.
Free rides don't exist.
Get it done.
Have confidence that you can make a difference.
Invite constructive criticism.
Just doing enough to get by, won't get it done.
Keep from making excuses.
Listen, learn and always work to improve your mind.
Mean what you say, and say what you mean.
Never, ever give up on your dreams.
Only one person can control you and that is you.
Pray.
Quality not quantity.
Respect others.
Sometimes, slow down and smell the roses.
Treat others with respect and they will respect you.
Use your assets wisely.
Voice your opinions.

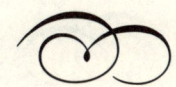

Work as hard as possible without forgetting your loved ones.
Xpect obstacles but accept challenges.
You are in charge of your own actions.
Zap obstacles and reach for the stars.

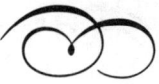

Your Work

Fall in love with your job and keep the romance alive.

Don't let the stress of change drive a wedge between you and your work. Sure, your employer will benefit if you are committed, but not as much as you will.

High job commitment is a gift you should give to yourself.

"I started out with nothing,
and I still have most of it."
— *Michael Davis,* The Tonight Show

Stop Thinking Tiny Thoughts

One of the timeless truths of successful living can be stated simply:
Your thoughts form your world.
What you focus on in your life grows.
What you think about expands.
What you dwell on determines your destiny.

The British Statesman Benjamin Disraeli once said:
"Nurture your mind with great thoughts,
for you will never go any higher than you think."

His words are profound and his point of wisdom is clear. It is not what you are that is holding you back in life. It is what you think you are not. It is what is going on in your inner world that is preventing you from having all that you want.
    The moment you fully understand this insight and set about ridding your mind of all its limiting thoughts, you will experience almost immediate improvements in your personal circumstances.

Learning From Noah's Ark

1. Don't miss the boat!
2. Remember that we are all in the same boat.
3. Plan ahead. It wasn't raining when Noah built the Ark.
4. Stay fit. When you're 600 years old, someone may ask you to do something really big.
5. Don't listen to critics; just get on with the job that needs to be done.
6. Build your future on high ground.
7. For safety's sake, travel in pairs.
8. Speed isn't always an advantage. The snails were on board with the cheetahs.
9. When you're stressed, float awhile.
10. Remember, the Ark was built by amateurs; the Titanic by professionals.
11. No matter the storm, when you are with God, there is always a rainbow waiting.

Excuses

Excuses benefit nobody — learn to take responsibility.

It's easy to make excuses, but when you look back upon them, they sound a little ridiculous. Take, for example, these descriptions of auto accidents turned in by insurance policy holders:

"The telephone pole was approaching fast. I was attempting to swerve out of its path when it struck my front end."

"I had been shopping for plants all day, and was on my way home. As I reached an intersection, a hedge sprang up obscuring my vision and I did not see the other car."

"I had been driving my car for four years when I fell asleep at the wheel and had an accident."

"I was on my way to the doctor's with rear end trouble when my universal joint gave way, causing me to have an accident."

Excuses only waste time and weaken your team's spirit. Begin now to take responsibility for your actions. If you make a mistake, set an example by "fessing up" and moving on to what needs to be done.

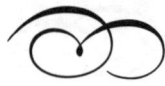

I Walk With . . .

At a recent speakers' conference in San Francisco, one of the keynote speakers was John Foppe who was born with no arms. His story and triumph is very compelling. He ends each speech with the following:

As I step into today's journey,
I walk with . . .
The vision of HOPE that gives meaning and direction to my steps.
The calmness of PATIENCE that helps me distinguish the pitfalls from solid ground.
The grit of PERSEVERANCE that enables me to stand up again after I have fallen.
The intimacy of PRAYER that assures me I do not walk down this path alone.

— *John P. Foppe*

Important Words to Remember

The six most important words: "I admit that I was wrong."
The five most important words: "You did a great job!"
The four most important words: "What do you think?"
The three most important words: "Could you please . . ."
The two most important words: "Thank you"
The most important word: "We"
The least important word: "I"
— *From* The Hospitality Jungle, *Max Hitchins*

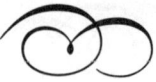

Resolutions

No one gets out of this world alive.

Resolve, therefore, to maintain a sense of values.

Take care of yourself. Good health is everyone's major source of wealth. Without it happiness is virtually impossible.

Resolve to be cheerful and helpful. People will repay in kind.

Avoid zealots. They are generally humourless.

Resolve to listen more and talk less. No one ever learns anything by talking.

Be wary of giving advice. Wise men don't need it, and fools won't heed it.

Resolve to be tender with the young, compassionate with the aged, sympathetic with the striving, and tolerant of the weak and wrong.

Sometimes in life you have to do all of these.

Do not equate money with success. The world abounds with big moneymakers who are miserable failures as human beings. What counts most about success is how a person achieves it.

The Time Management Profile

Voltaire, the great French writer and philosopher, posed an interesting question in his book *Zadig: A Mystery of Fate*.

The Grand Magi asked Zadig, "What, of all things in the world, is the longest and the shortest, the swiftest and the slowest, the most divisible and the most extended, the most neglected and the most regretted, without which nothing can be done, which devours all that is little and enlivens all that is great?"

Without hesitation, Zadig answered, "Time."
He added:

- Nothing is longer, since it is the measure of eternity.
- Nothing is shorter, since it is insufficient for the accomplishment of our projects.
- Nothing is more slow to him that expects; nothing more rapid to him that enjoys.
- In greatness, it extends to infinity; in smallness, it is infinitely divisible.
- All men neglect it; all regret the loss of it; nothing can be done without it.
- It consigns to oblivion whatever is unworthy of being transmitted to posterity, and it immortalizes such actions as are truly great.

Risking

Two seeds lay side by side in the fertile spring soil. The first seed said, "I want to grow! I want to send my roots deep into the soil beneath me, and thrust my sprouts through the earth's crust above me . . . I want to feel the warmth of the sun on my face and the blessing of the morning dew on my petals!"

And so she grew.

The second seed said, "I'm afraid. If I send my roots into the ground below, I don't know what I will find in the dark. If I push my way through the hard soil above me I may damage my delicate sprouts. It's much better for me to wait until it is safe."

And so she waited.

In the early spring, a hen scratching around for food found the waiting seed and promptly ate it.

Moral:
Those of us who refuse to risk and grow get swallowed up by life.

— *Patty Hansen*

Always Remember

Always remember to forget,
The things that make you sad,
But never forget the things that make you glad.
Always remember to forget,
The friends that proved untrue.
But don't forget to remember,
Those who have stuck by you.
Always remember to forget,
The troubles that passed away,
But never forget to remember
The blessings that come each day.

The Wise One

In the city of Baghdad lived Hakeem; the Wise One and many people went to him for counsel, which he gave freely to all, asking nothing in return.

There came to him a young man who had spent much but gotten little, who said, "Tell me, Wise One, what should I do to receive the most for that which I spend?"

Hakeem answered, "A thing that is bought or sold has no value unless it contains that which cannot be bought or sold. Look for the priceless ingredient."

"But what is the priceless ingredient?" asked the young man.

Spoke the Wise One, "My son, the priceless ingredient of every product on the marketplace is the honour and integrity of him who makes it. Consider his name before you buy."

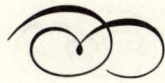

Special Notes to Special Friends

Many people will walk in and out of your life,
But only true friends will leave footprints in your heart.
To handle yourself, use your head,
To handle others, use your heart.
Anger is only one letter short of danger.
If someone betrays you once, it is his fault;
If he betrays you twice, it is your fault.
Great minds discuss ideas,
Average minds discuss events,
Small minds discuss people.
He who loses money, loses much;
He who loses a friend, loses much more;
He who loses faith, loses all.
Learn from the mistakes of others.
You can't live long enough to make them all yourself.
Friends, you and me . . .
You brought another friend . . .
And then there were three . . .
We started our group . . .
Our circle of friends . . .
And like that circle . . .
There is no beginning or end.

The $20 Dollar Bill

A well-known speaker started off his seminar by holding up a $20 bill. In the room of 200, he asked, "Who would like this $20 bill?" Hands started going up.

He said, "I am going to give this $20 to one of you but first let me do this." He proceeded to crumple the bill up.

He then asked, "Who still wants it?" Still the hands were up in the air. "Well," he replied, "What if I do this?" And he dropped it on the ground and started to grind it into the floor with his shoe. He picked it up, now all crumpled and dirty. "Now who still wants it?" Still the hands went into the air.

"My friends, you have all learned a very valuable lesson. No matter what I did to the money, you still wanted it because it did not decrease in value. It was still worth $20."

Many times in our lives, we are dropped, crumpled and ground into the dirt by the decisions we make and the circumstances that come our way. We feel as though we are worthless. But no matter what has happened or what will happen, you will never lose your value.

You are special! Don't ever forget it!

Never let yesterday's disappointments overshadow tomorrow's dreams.

The Garden

A person's mind is like a garden; it can be intelligently cultivated or allowed to run wild. Whether cultivated or neglected, it is visible for all to see.

Just as a gardener cultivates their land, keeping it free from weeds, and growing flowers and fruits, so may a person tend the garden of their mind.

It is important to weed out all the inappropriate, useless and tainted thoughts. Take time to cultivate honest, useful and reasonable thoughts. Plant with the seeds of knowledge for new growth.

You can be the master gardener of your soul, the director of your life. It is your thoughts and mind, which shape your character, circumstances and destiny.

— *James Allen*

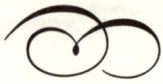

The Failure List

Einstein was four years old before he could speak.

Isaac Newton did poorly in grade school and was considered "unpromising."

Beethoven's music teacher once said of him, "As a composer, he is hopeless."

When Thomas Edison was a youngster, his teacher told him he was too stupid to learn anything. He was counseled to go into a field where he might succeed by virtue of his pleasant personality.

F.W. Woolworth got a job in a dry goods store when he was 21, but his employer would not permit him to wait on customers because he "didn't have enough sense to close a sale."

Michael Jordan was cut from his high school basketball team.

Boston Celtics Hall of Famer Bob Cousy suffered the same fate.

A newspaper editor fired Walt Disney because he "lacked imagination and had no good ideas."

Winston Churchill had to repeat Grade 6 because he did not complete the tests that were required for promotion.

Babe Ruth struck out 1,300 times — a major league record.

A person may make mistakes, but isn't a failure until he or she starts blaming someone else. We must believe in ourselves, and somewhere along the road of life, we must meet someone who sees greatness in us, expects it from us, and lets us know it. It is the golden key to success.

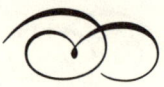

The Challenge

Let others lead small lives,
   but not you.
Let others argue over small things,
   but not you.
Let others cry over small hurts,
   but not you.
Let others leave their future
   in someone else's hands,
   but not you.

— *Jim Rohn*

My Parachute

Charles Plumb was a U.S. Navy jet pilot in Vietnam. After 75 combat missions his plane was destroyed by a surface to air missile. Plumb ejected and parachuted into enemy territory. He was captured and spent six years in a Communist Vietnamese prison. He survived that ordeal and now lectures on lessons learned by that ordeal.

One day when Plumb and his wife were seated in a restaurant, a man from another table came over and said, "You're Plumb, you flew jet fighters from the aircraft *Kitty Hawk*, you were shot down." "How in the world did you know that?" asked Plumb. "I packed your parachute," the man replied. Plumb gasped in surprise and gratitude. The man pumped his hand and said, "I guess it worked." Plumb assured him that it surely did, otherwise he wouldn't be here today.

Plumb couldn't sleep that night, thinking about that man. Plumb says he kept wondering what he would have looked like in a Navy uniform, a white hat, a bib in the back and bell bottom trousers. "I wonder how many times I might have seen him and not even said good morning, how are you or anything. Because you see I was an officer and a fighter pilot and he was just a sailor." Plumb thought of the many hours the sailor had spent at a long wooden table in the bowels of that ship, carefully weaving the shrouds and folding the silk

of each chute, holding in his hands each time the fate of someone he didn't know.

Now Plumb asks his audience, "Who is packing your parachute?" Everyone has someone who provides what they need to make it through the day. He also points out that he needed many kinds of parachutes when his plane went down over enemy territory — he needed his physical parachute, his emotional parachute, his spiritual parachute. He called on all of these supports before reaching safety.

Sometimes in the daily challenges that life gives us, we miss what is really important. We may fail to say hello, please or thank you, congratulate someone on something wonderful that has happened to them, give a compliment or just do something nice for no reason. As you go through this week, this month, this year, recognize the people who pack your parachutes.

Images of Father

Age 4   "My daddy can do anything!"

Age 8   "My dad knows a lot! A whole lot!"

Age 12   "My father doesn't really know quite everything."

Age 14   "Naturally father doesn't know that either!"

Age 16   "Father? He's hopelessly old-fashioned."

Age 18   "He's way out of date."

Age 25   "Well, he might know a little bit about it."

Age 35   "Before we decide, let's get dad's opinion."

Age 45   "Wonder what dad would've thought about it."

Age 65   "Wish I could talk it over with dad."

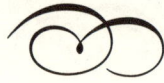

I will persist until I succeed.

I will persist until I succeed.

I will never consider defeat and I will remove from my vocabulary such words and phrases as quit, cannot, unable, impossible, out of the question, improbable, failure, unworkable, hopeless and retreat; for they are the words of fools.

I will avoid despair but if this disease of the mind should infect me then I will work on in despair. I will toil and I will endure. I will ignore the obstacles at my feet and keep mine eyes on the goals above my head, for I know that where dry desert ends, green grass grows.

— *Excerpt from* The Greatest Salesman in the World
by Og Mandino

Words to think about

"It is one of the strange ironies of this strange life that those who work the hardest, who subject themselves to the strictest discipline, who give up certain pleasurable things in order to achieve a goal, are the happiest people. When you see 20 or 30 people line up for a distance race in some meet, don't pity them, don't feel sorry for them. Better envy them instead."
— *Brutus Hamilton, placed second in the 1920 Olympic decathlon and sixth in the pentathlon, and went on to coach track at the University of California in Berkeley for 33 years.*

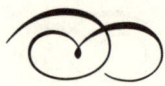

Rules for Living

Do not worry,
eat three square meals a day,
say your prayers,
be courteous to your creditors,
keep your digestion good,
steer clear of biliousness,
exercise,
go slow and go easy.

Maybe there are
other things that
your special case requires to
make you happy, but, my friend,
these, I reckon,
will give you a good life.

— *Abraham Lincoln*

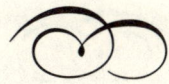

A Magic Way of Going

1. Be generous in your praise and support of others.
2. Forgiveness is freedom. Put your hate, anger and revenge in the garbage can where they belong.
3. Learn to think creatively. Solutions live in your imagination.
4. See life positively. Every problem is an opportunity for those with eyes to see.
5. There is no growth without pain. Birds always sing after the rain.
6. Be grateful for your gifts, your country, and for those you love.
7. Value the magic in each other.
8. Learn to laugh at life and at yourself. Most of what you worry about will still be here long after you are gone.
9. Find time to do the things you love. Develop a wish list and start checking it off. This moment is all you have.
10. Be considerate, caring and honest in everything you say and do. Your epitaph is being written today.

You are not dust, you're magic.

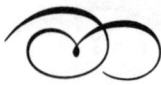

All You Can

Do all the good you can,
In all the ways you can,
To all the souls you can,
In every place you can,
At all the times you can,
With all the zeal you can,
As long as ever you can.

— *John Wesley*

Make Your Plans

Make your plans
as fantastic as you like,
because 25 years from now,
they will seem mediocre.

Make your plans 10 times
as great as you first planned,
and 25 years from now
you will wonder why you did
not make them 50
times as great.

— *Henry Curtis*

We overestimate what we can achieve in one year but we underestimate what we can achieve in five years.

— *Peter Drucker*

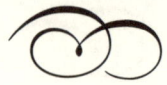

About the Author

Dr. Peter Legge, LL.D (HON) • CSP • CPAE

Peter Legge is President and CEO of Canada Wide Magazines & Communications Ltd., the largest independently owned publishing company in Western Canada, controlling a network of 17 magazines across the country with over $25 million in sales annually.

In addition, Peter travels the world as a motivational speaker, accepting more than 100 assignments each year from clients who know that when he speaks, his words will be a catalyst for positive change. He has received the prestigious Golden Gavel Award from Toastmasters International and was voted "Top Speaker in North America," in company with Dr. Robert Schuller and Stephen Covey. Peter has also been inducted into the Speakers Hall of Fame by both the National Speakers Association and the Canadian Association of Professional Speakers.

Peter is tireless in his commitments to many worthwhile organizations. As co-host of the annual Variety Club Telethon for more than 20 years, he has assisted in raising more than $75 million for the charity. He is also an International Ambassador of Variety Clubs International.

His efforts have not gone unnoticed. Among his many honours, Peter has received the Golden Heart Award from the Variety Club and has been invested into the Venerable Order of St. John of Jerusalem. He has been awarded the Order of the Red Cross and named Citizen of the Year for his commitment to the community. Simon Fraser University recently honoured him with an Honorary Doctor of Laws Degree, and he is the current Chair of the Vancouver Board of Trade.

Peter is also the author of five previous books that have inspired thousands of readers the world over with their powerful motivating messages. In all that he has achieved, Peter attributes his success to three factors: persistence, patience and a positive attitude.

To contact Peter Legge, write to:
Peter Legge Management Company,
4180 Lougheed Highway, 4th Floor
Burnaby, B.C. V5C 6A7
Canada
Telephone: 604-299-7311
E-mail plegge@canadawide.com

The quotes, insights and maxims assembled in *If Only I'd Said That: Volume II* have been collected over a lifetime and are meant to be shared with others so that they may inspire, uplift and enrich their lives. Many of these quotes are unknown to me. Should you know the source of the unattributed quotes in this book, I would be indebted to you if you would write to me so that I may attach proper credit in future editions. Similarly, should a quote be wrongfully attributed, I would be grateful to know of the original author so that he or she may be duly acknowledged.

Peter Legge